# THE FILMS OF WOODY ALLEN

# THE FILMS OF WOODY ALLEN

## Robert Benayoun
Translated by Alexander Walker

Harmony Books / New York

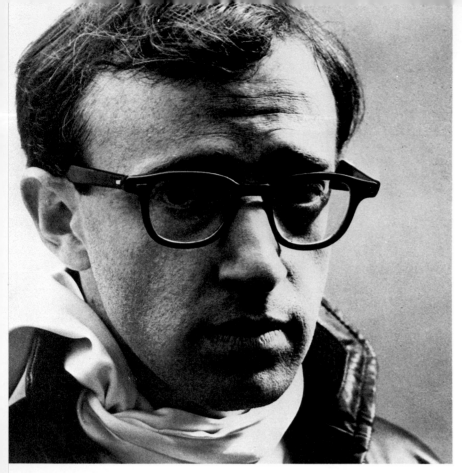

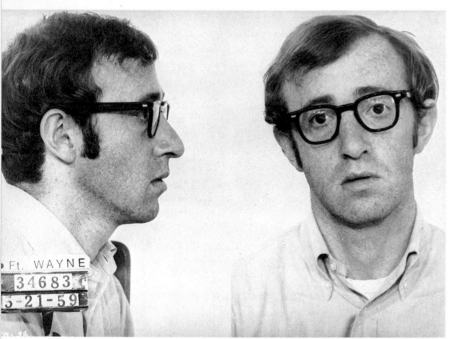

6

Saul Steinberg once drew a famous and cynical comment on 'America'. It showed in the foreground a clutter of New York's familiar – over-familiar – landmarks. And then, beyond, looking westward, there was a great expanse of flatness almost devoid of distinguishing features until the spectator's eye reached the Pacific coast. The parochial, in other words, is often the mote in the eye that should be taking in the continental perspective.

That way is how one sometimes feels Woody Allen is regarded by those who speak the English language and relish American humour, particularly the kind that holds the joyous apprehension of the Jewish experience in its cadences and observations. We see Woody too clearly against his own background: he is so familiar, so native a landmark that we don't bother to look at the setting; we feel we know the 'neighbourhood'. It is a friendly, a folksy approach to one of the best-loved clowns in the world and certainly the most original artist currently working in the American cinema: but it is a deceptive perspective to see Woody Allen as only an American humourist. This is where Robert Benayoun's book presents an invaluable corrective.

For what this French critic has done is sneak past us, round to the other side of Woody, so to speak, and view him against a European light; and the critical illumination that falls on Woody is a transfiguring one indeed, yet as attractive as it is startling.

It's not simply that Benayoun's intellectual credentials are wider than those which most Anglo-Saxon film critics think it necessary to possess for the job (or, possessing them, to exercise in the job), although it's perfectly true to say that a film like *Interiors*, for example, has seldom had the scale of its ambitions so rigorously classified by the American or British critics. Yes, we all saw the 'Bergman connection'. But how many of us noticed that Woody's aspirations were fed by such artists as Emil Nolde and Edvard Munch? Not intellectual guess-work, either: for Benayoun spies a Nolde among the paintings that Woody has collected on his penthouse walls; and he knows, as well as the film-maker himself, that all one has to do is look into the print room at the Museum of Modern Art to find hanging on the wall that self-same engraving by Edvard Munch whose bleak grouping of funereal figures is reproduced with such exactness in the movie. Likewise, *A Midsummer Night's Sex Comedy* may have been mainly a Woody Allen 'entertainment' set, for once, in the countryside, not the city, hence seductive and relaxed rather than angst-ridden. Yes, we all got the 'Renoir connection'. But it is Benayoun who justly appreciates the resemblance between Woody's little rural jack-of-all-trades in the film, one of those pioneer inventors who have given American science its individualistic energy, and an artist-innovator like Joseph Wright of Derby whose own paintings of country barns have the same interior radiance that Woody's film reproduces in its bucolic locations.

There is an astringent pleasure in seeing cross-cultural references applied appositely and revealingly to an American film-maker whose own intellectual stamina was never in doubt, but who has frequently met with resistance from those of his countrymen who bit the hand that fed them jokes whenever they detected it dabbling in more 'serious' matters such as its owner's right to self-expression. Benayoun is a champion of the artist's search for maturity; and he is at pains to remind us that the off-screen Woody is not at all the same character that we see on it – or not *entirely*. Read the transcript of the conversations he has held with Woody at one time and another: the sobriety is astonishing, as well as the insight.

I suspect this refreshing seriousness is partly a response to the sober line of questioning Benayoun pursued. Most people who interview Woody, the Frenchman correctly asserts, would go away disappointed if the comic denied them what they'd come to expect from him as he appears 'in character' on the screen. I can speak from personal experience. I once spent a couple of entertaining hours with Woody Allen, during which I've never known one man's troubles to sound so funny – to someone else, anyhow. We had got on to a relationship that Benayoun examines in some detail in the book, when he notes how, like other clowns such as Charlie Chaplin, Woody's affairs with the opposite sex are stimulating, in the creative sense, too. *Annie Hall* and *Manhattan* are anthologies of real-life love affairs – and infinitely more complex, more 'adult' than any other screen comic had allowed himself to have in his films. Like Bergman, Woody pondered on what could be done with all the women who appeared to collect around him. 'Can't you refer them to an analyst?' I asked him facetiously . . . and suddenly he had become the little guy with the emotional heartburn and the line in sappy patter that he knew I was expecting: 'Oh, sure . . . I suppose I could do that. But then you cease to be a lover. You become the Jewish voice of reason. Here is this girl vowing to set herself on fire for you and all you can find to say is, "You really ought to see a doctor." '

Benayoun would not have let him get away with that: one of the most attractive features of his study is the emotional maturity he recognizes exists in his subject and the generosity, even, with which Woody has been able to articulate it, by transforming his real-life girlfriends into creations who are part of his world yet independent of him – like the deliciously daffy, chicly dishevelled Annie Hall. Yet even his success in attracting women has occasionally invited the critical backlash from those who don't find it credible that someone who looks like Woody Allen could score so often. It's a charge that Benayoun – who, after all, comes from the country that produced Cyrano – is able to rebut with some asperity and even to show how the implication that one had to be a Robert Redford to be sexually appealing was turned to creative advantage in Woody Allen's subsequent work.

Benayoun has no diffidence, either, in assigning Woody his place in the extraordinary diaspora of Jewish clowns; even though Woody protests that his humour is not 'typically Jewish', I think the justness of Benayoun's observation and the detailed lineage provided for it are undeniable. 'Torn between the Hebrew language that he can't learn and the Borscht Belt jokes that make him ashamed and all those English phrases he

# INTRODUCTION

envies in his literary models – Robert Benchley, for example
– [Woody)]invents a bizarre defence system for himself, a
complex structure of observations about each and
everything. . . . Everything that he was ever afraid of learning
about racism [and wanted not to know)] Woody reveals it.'
Incidentally, Benayoun errs only in fact, not sympathetic affili-
ation, when he classifies Charlie Chaplin as Jewish; for as David
Robinson's recent definitive study conclusively established,
Chaplin had no Jewish blood, yet he felt such spiritual kinship
with the race that when he was accused of belonging to it by
the Nazis he preferred his silence to be taken as an acknow-
legement rather than have his denial misinterpreted as dissociating himself from the great suffering of the Jews and the stoic
wit that is their hereditary compensation. 'Humour for Woody
remains a Jewish prerogative.' Of course, there's always been
an American tradition that comics are natural philosophers. But
as this study brings out so shrewdly and literately, no other
philosopher in America has learned how to *worry* his way into
life as well as Woody Allen. Most philosophers seem somewhat
above life and therefore, I suspect, miss a lot of its funny, crazy
texture – possibly (as Woody himself might say) that's why
Kierkegaard is not a riot of laughs. But Woody Allen, a serious
man when it comes to catching the anxieties that haunt us all,
has also time for the small zaniness let loose in the cosmos that
takes the pressure off – at least for as long as it takes to tell
the joke. In Robert Benayoun, he has found a defender of the
faith as well as a companionable analyst.

Alexander Walker

'Spinoza is the only person who may not have read Spinoza.'

**Francis Picabia**

'I don't want to gain immortality in my works. I want to gain it by not dying.'

**Woody Allen**

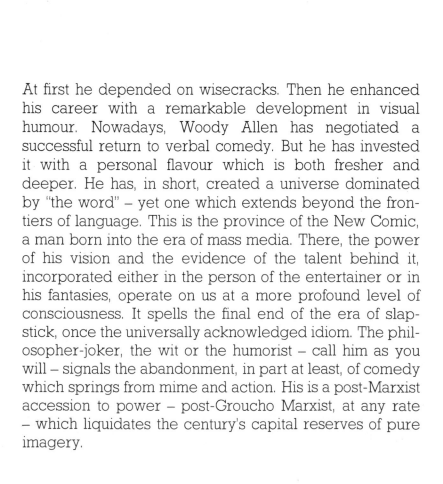

At first he depended on wisecracks. Then he enhanced his career with a remarkable development in visual humour. Nowadays, Woody Allen has negotiated a successful return to verbal comedy. But he has invested it with a personal flavour which is both fresher and deeper. He has, in short, created a universe dominated by "the word" – yet one which extends beyond the frontiers of language. This is the province of the New Comic, a man born into the era of mass media. There, the power of his vision and the evidence of the talent behind it, incorporated either in the person of the entertainer or in his fantasies, operate on us at a more profound level of consciousness. It spells the final end of the era of slapstick, once the universally acknowledged idiom. The philosopher-joker, the wit or the humorist – call him as you will – signals the abandonment, in part at least, of comedy which springs from mime and action. His is a post-Marxist accession to power – post-Groucho Marxist, at any rate – which liquidates the century's capital reserves of pure imagery.

WA-F-21

It's a common characteristic of celebrity to give rise to a curious syndrome in the world of show-business, namely identifying the actor with the role he plays. Some roles brand a player indelibly, however he resists it, forcing on him an image that's sometimes the opposite of his temperament or his real nature. This misleading impression is one that he is going to have to efface some time or other if he is to reinvent his career – his own very existence – with that ebb and flow that free will provides for. Such a man needs great courage, a certain sense of what it takes to say No to the god called Success, by taking himself in hand and going against the collective image that the media have sanctioned. He needs to have a clear idea of what he wants to be, even though it may conflict with what destiny orders him to remain.

This is even truer for comic artists who have created a fully rounded personality for themselves over the years, one easily identifiable by costume, accessories, gestures or voice.

For fifty years Chaplin, a master of the cinema, who set up his own company and built his own studios, a Don Juan in his own right and worshipped by the intelligentsia, projected the image of an uneducated tramp disregarded by women. But once he disavowed it, he incurred the righteous indignation of his fans, who couldn't bear the idea of the man who had killed off Charlie putting a crease in his trousers and yielding place to Verdoux, *Limelight*'s Calvero and *The Great Dictator*'s Hynkel. The image that had already been created was so potent that he had the greatest difficulty overlaying it with other ones, like the man who laid romantic siege to widows and then murdered them, or the tyrant out of Nietzsche.

Stan Laurel, up against his overbearing partner, pulling his forelock with a despairing gesture, whingeing or losing his temper, all the better to suggest a fractious child, gave an impression of meekness and mildness which was belied (and this, too, was also like something he affected) by a deep bass voice. One now knows that, of the two partners, he was the stronger-willed, a perfectionist and quite a megalomaniac.

Harry Langdon, with his baby's face that looked as if it had just been sprinkled with talc and smiling like a child being suckled, acted like an eternal infant. But behind that moon-struck clown's face with its touching wistfulness there lurked a neurotic temperament given to bouts of manic-depression.

Harold Lloyd, for his part, with his straw boater and beaming smile, projected a healthy, go-getting personality which, in the America of Horatio Alger and Dale Carnegie, embodied everyone's dream of success to such an extent that, unlike his peers, he had no need of any other surname to identify him: relishing his anonymity, he became the man who in Europe was called quite simply – 'He'.

It's as if the thankless trade of being a 'clown', which one knows burdens a comic with a weight of loneliness and alienation, were requiring him to resort, temporarily anyhow, to wearing a mask: some time or other, the itch comes to tear it off and show one's real face.

Such a phenomenon resembles what has happened to Woody Allen.

When his moment came he won a place among the greatest in the cinema's golden age of comedy by creating the image of an insecure intellectual: maladroit, accident prone, at odds with the world of machines and unlucky in the realm of love. But such a self-imposed personality, as we shall see, had little connection with the person he wanted to be from childhood – a figure who, one day, would share the peak of success alongside the other.

The truth is that every study of him, every book and article on Allen customarily begins with a portrait of the character he plays, *not* the actor himself. It's usually a physical description: his clothes, his hair, his attitude of so-called *schlemiel* at odds with a hostile environment. Such a picture, of course, derives from particular roles that Woody Allen has played in different films, but it doesn't correspond to real life.

The characterization of him, as thorough as any dictionary of emotional neuroses, has little bearing on what follows. His features are at once sad, dreamy and resigned; his watery eyes look out through thick black-framed glasses at a world that has been 'against' him from birth; his sparse yet curly hair seems to have been dried with a flame-thrower; his thick, stammering lips disappear into a sad crease; his stubby, puny, ill-favoured body suggests the botched job of an absent-minded Frankenstein, an image which, as we shall see, has haunted his many fantasies. The people who write about him stress such characteristics, which can easily turn into carica-ture (though one he has certainly authorized). It's that of the comic who has intentionally made himself appear more and more insignificant ever since his first professional appear-ances. It was in night-clubs that such an image took shape – irreversible now, perhaps – of a perennially balding short-sighted and untidy fellow. One needs a bestiary to contain the multitude of analogies he has inspired. At one and the same time he has been an owl, a 'harassed sparrow', a little mole, a 'rabbit in flight', a 'shrimp out of water grappling with the absurdity of modern life', a 'little mouse in eye-glasses', a 'lemur with bitten finger-nails', a 'hermit crab', and so on. Some of his critics see him as an 'archetypal bungler', to quote James Monaco, an 'imperfectionist', the 'urban boychik as social misfit', a 'half-pint of neuroses', a 'moaner and groaner' or 'the Samson of the sad sacks'.

The character he plays, although kept at arm's length by a Woody who resists any quick or simple analysis, is often involved in, or made responsible for, the very reactions that he himself arouses in people. He is accused of being too calculatingly laid back, of perversely harping on and on about his inability to come to terms with life. Some very far-fetched charges are laid against him: that he is 'stupefyingly ordinary', 'aggressively unkempt', extravagantly meek and mild, and impossibly moody.

Yet how can one fail to see that this creation is over-shadowed, obliterated and rendered obsolete by the dynamic Woody, getting up to his tricks and recounting his adventures. One knows that Woody Allen is good at sports; one knows that he possesses great manual dexterity (he's mastered sleight of hand); and one can't ignore his seductive power – a peculiar kind, certainly – based on a fairly intellectual appeal, yet

Conquest of the space
beyond the words **PREFACE**

sufficiently potent to have him shadowed along the pavements like a pop idol by the *paparazzi* and the autograph hunters.

There is also – a godsend to gossip writers! – his talent for being endlessly, almost excessively quotable. Some articles that have appeared on him are shameless collages of his own *bons mots* and aphorisms, slightly altered or condensed, in which his opinions are wrenched out of context and crudely misrepresented by somewhat unscrupulous 'admirers'. The commonest example of this – one has kept coming across it for the last five years or so – is the phrase 'His one regret in life is that he is not someone else.' Written by Woody as a joke, the problem is that it was taken too seriously and keeps on coming back to him like a boomerang. It is reproduced, with his permission of course, in every one of his publishers' blurbs, so much so that it is now part of the myth: This phrase, popping up like a rabbit out of a top hat, usually elicits a condescending response from the customary chorus of sceptics, such as : 'We just want him to stay himself.' That sort of opinion is no easier to live with than if one were confined inside a tight collar, a suit that has shrunk or a doll's house.

In extreme cases Woody Allen inspires imitation, provokes his critics almost to acts of unintentional osmosis. The parody essayist sees *himself* being parodied by facile imitators who believe they can size up his talent, or cut it *down* to size, with what comes quickest to him and in the most inimitable fashion – his own style. Catching this kind of infection – almost as indecent as it is embarrassing – some of his interviewers ask him questions that try to be funny. They encourage him to fence with them verbally and so excel himself, or so they hope. He didn't play the game with his interrogators from *Playboy*, who parodied him while putting together their own worthless life story; nor with the critics of *Time* or *Newsweek* who indulged in pathetic puns: one of them, referring to *Broadway Danny Rose*, informed us that Mia Farrow, who was playing an Italian girl, had a hair-do like a 'Leaning Tower of Pizza'; the other magazine, apropos of the same film, talked of 'pastrami-on-wry', which hardly showed more inventiveness. It's as if an irresistible word-fever grips everyone coming into contact with him.

When people used to write about the great names in comedy they had at the very least the duty to describe the mime they used, their body language, the quirks and mannerisms. This occasionally obliged them to make slight adjustments to their own methods of description. It's hard to convey in writing, in any meaningful way, what a slow burn is like, or a double take, or any other simple action. Writers today have an easier task with Groucho Marx or Woody Allen: all they do is quote the dialogue while referring to the story: which permits them to reduce their own labours by a sizeable amount. Other rather cheekier commentators simply paraphrase him (or come close to doing so and fall into banality.

In analysing him, one has to ask oneself whether Woody Allen hasn't evolved his comic image out of the pure slapstick era based on physical expression and actions in the more or less violent tradition that stretches from Mack Sennett to Hal Roach (or from Chaplin to Laurel and Hardy) and into an era of verbal virtuosity carried to the ends of the earth by satellite and characterized by television's situation comedies, stand-up comedians and gag-merchants who are to be found almost everywhere, from Mort Sahl and Lenny Bruce to Bob Hope, Johnny Carson, Don Rickles or Richard Pryor.

To the present-day 'audio-visual generation', saturated with images, transfixed by the Medusa-like video clips of Michael

*Play It Again, Sam* (page 12 and above)

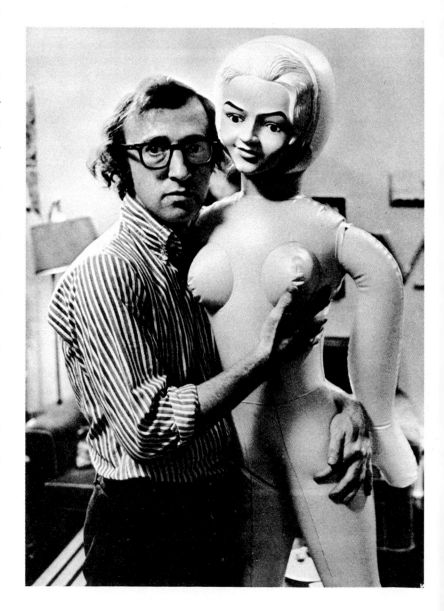

14

Jackson, Elton John or David Bowie, Woody Allen looks like one of those faces which stands out among the crowd of imagery by the cathartic power of what they signify.

Our epoch, more than any other, is one in which the spoken word forces itself to the fore, imposes itself on our consciousness and orders our life with the dispassionate power of a natural law. Woody seduces us by his delivery, his pauses, his reprises, his timing. The *mot juste*, arriving on the dot, caps the visual image, as if constituting the chapter heading, the picture caption, the aside or the ad lib.

Woody Allen is one of those who can create stunning imagery, freshly minted analogies that admit no contradiction, dazzling improvisations that query all that seems safest in our world. He is an eloquent master of the well-observed incongruity, flowing easily in and out of matter-of-fact chat and freewheeling improvisation. His specific appeal isn't apparent in his gaze; for unlike Buster Keaton, short-sighted Woody allows a wild, unfocused, vacancy to be clearly visible through his thick glasses, rarely looking at the camera, even during his monologues, or else doing so stealthily, with unease or embarrassment. It lies in the words he uses, the way he loads them with perpetual references to himself, as if nothing had any relevance except when refracted through the prism of his own peculiar way of regarding things.

He is a striking paradox, this cinema hero, occasionally a star of the cabaret stage, but a man who belongs first and foremost within the frame of the cinema screen. Like a watermark within it as well as an image on it, he focuses our attention by a mode of speech that he has made all his own. He has multiplied himself in words in many different media: he has parcelled them into slim volumes which he has published at intervals, satirical essays in magazines, then into a sort of running commentary that regularly reverberates from one film to the next, expanding and overlapping in successive waves. Notwithstanding his sure mastery of the image, which he wooed and tamed after a lengthy courtship, he remains a man who relies on words.* Without trying to put over a message, words flow out of him in arabesque patterns: a stream of free-flowing conversation that carries him anywhere and everywhere.

He has loved words from childhood. They have shaped his life, given existence to his work – they're inseparable from his being. Words are his currency: the sentences he has shaped form the very bed he lies on .His writing is unique; and the scenarios he creates stand up to being re-read, in tranquillity and with pleasure. His written words have the happy knack of staying in one's mind and seeming even better when one reads them again. Now that his films are available for one's video library, the cassettes preserve them in unchanging form and one can refer to them the way that one re-reads Pagnol or Guitry, with the feeling that one will never forget a single twist or turn in them, that one will never grow tired of savouring them: they are like W. C. Fields's short, *The Fatal Glass of Beer*, or the card party in Pagnol's *Marius*, or the stateroom scene in the Marx Brothers, *Night at the Opera*; or Ionesco's *The Bald Soprano*. They are things of perpetual pleasure; our children will still be talking about them half a century from now. But even more, they are films made for the bookshelves:

they should be published so as to comprise a sort of bible, in uniform bindings like the volumes of the Pleiade series in France. And I hardly need add that *Manhattan* and *Annie Hall* stand 're-reading' better than Paul Claudel, and have more point.

Note that Woody is the only comic in the history of the cinema whose dialogue, with all its nuances, needs to be heard in the original English – not dubbed – and this applies even to those who don't speak English and depend on the sub-titles. It doesn't matter too much that a lot of him is lost in translation, particularly in the sub-titling: dubbing, on the other hand, constitutes, as always, the ultimate betrayal. His choice of language – precise, compact, comprising many aphorisms – needs twice as many words in French as in English. It is the same with Coleridge, Edward Lear or Cole Porter.

Woody's monologues on disc provide the polyglot peoples of Europe with a better lesson in vocal rhythm and the feeling for cadence than any casette orf conversational English from language schools or any of the simultaneous translations at the UN. His is a unique form of Esperanto.

It is worth noting that among the great auteurs whom Woody admires, or translates into his own idiom, like Fellini, Bergman and others I particularly admire, like Renais, Antonioni and Huston, a similar consistency of tone finds pride of place. The director stays faithful to himself throughout a diverse career, whether engaged in risky or prestigious undertakings or going in for creative experiment. Woody, on the other hand, uses film for the purpose of dissembling himself. His films spread out in all directions, in the way his own gaze used to do. He functions like a stiff clutch which suddenly frees itself in the course of acceleration; whereupon, unhindered, he can pursue his experiments in all directions, some of them seemingly contradictory. The proof of him is to be found in his *diversity*.

One final remark:

At the time this book was written, Woody had directed barely fourteen films, though his influence had been visible on innumerable others and had thus changed the course and the tone of American movie comedy. (Let it be enough to remember what cinema talents like Marshall Brickman, Paul Mazursky and Alan Alda owe him.) It would seem, therefore, that Woody's verbal abundance has inspired plenty of other people's and indeed words surround him as profusely as in his own screenplays and collected writings: six books on him have already been published in English, others have appeared in other languages. (See the bibliography in this book.)

To sum up, Woody is far from the end of an *oeuvre* that many of us hope will be full of abundant surprises. Remarkably rich and original though they are, his films constitute only a 'work in progress', and one that is growing in complexity all the time.

What's to come is still in the planning stage and, urged on by us in our unreasonable and impatient way, Woody has many difficulties as well as achievements ahead of him, without becoming a prisoner of his own diffidence, doubts and desires.

The worship of fans and the scrutiny of critics mustn't put constraints on him. This book is a half-term report: one could entitle it *Woody Allen's Midsummer Film Study and Critical Commentary*, employing the same kind of provisional title that he does whenever he is shooting a new film. It's a report pro tem, an *aide-memoire*, which doesn't try to reach any definitive conclusions. For one mustn't jeopardize those tenuous currents of inspiration that support him, or his resilient energy, or obliterate the trails he has blazed for himself.

---

* And he remains so, even when he doesn't speak a word, whether he is on screen or off: what he has to say is then delegated to one of his favourite collaborators, who conveys it without the quality of the material or the conversation being affected: Louise Lasser, Diane Keaton and Tony Roberts often utter his best lines of dialogue by proxy.

Tantalizing Amazonian beauties, the prizes to be had at the top of the social ladder

**The rumpled hero:**
dumpy, trance-like, fixed
in a bemused stance
(Below: with Tony
Roberts).
*Play It Again, Sam*

Long before he gave his films their own distinctive look and had impressed on the affections of his huge public the key image of himself (a misleading one, as it turned out) of a rumpled and distraught hero which would secure him a place, a cranny, in the collective unconscious, Woody had been known as a 'voice', or, rather, a whole conversation piece. What's undeniable is that the 'word' came first.

Woody once told me: 'I've always had an extremely easy talent for writing. I was always the one who wrote essays at school and read them out loud in front of the class.'

One knows that, around 1953, encouraged by his teachers at Midwood High School in the suburb of Flatbush where his family was living, he began selling funny items, usually gags that took the form of an anecdote, to newspaper columnists like Earl Wilson; then to show-business people like Arthur Murray, Guy Lombardo or Sammy Kaye. Before long a press agent called David Alber started commissioning fifty or so gags a day at five dollars each. Woody used to write them on the subway between Brooklyn and Manhattan. Next this shy youth was writing for Sid Caesar's comedy show, earning more than $1500 a week and on the staff of the laughter team which included Carl Reiner, Neil Simon and Mel Brooks: the competition there was fierce. Sketches and jokes for Pat Boone, Buddy Hackett and Peter Lind Hayes followed.

Max Liebman, a founder of the legendary *Show of Shows*, wrote at this time: 'Woody Allen writes well *only for himself*. As a writer, he's a total professional, as a comic, he's an amateur.'

The diagnosis was cruel, but well based. It was at this time that Woody's agents, Jack Rollins and Charles Joffe, who have since become his producers, chose to reverse the process and push him to demonstrate his talent on the stage; and by 'push', I mean literally so; they often strong-armed him in front of the footlights – a terrified beginner. Woody's education was completed in the night-clubs of Manhattan.

The frightened fledgling, unprepared to leave the family nest at '1402 Avenue K' took courage from his undeniable gift for words. He began venturing outside his home territory, setting foot on the professional scene which he most dreaded, yet which was to have the most profound effect on him. Examining the account of his life that Woody so often purveyed illustrates the basic truth of this. Born in Flatbush, a heavily Jewish section of Brooklyn, into a lower class family, he was the son of Martin Konigsberg, who had been at one time or another an engraver of jewellery, a taxi driver and a waiter in an off-Broadway restaurant, and of Nettea Cherrie, a book keeper in a florist's. Allan Stewart Konigsberg, nicknamed 'Red' by his classmates on account of his red squirrel-like mop of hair, aroused the admiration of his fellow pupils, though not for excelling at his studies (according to his friend Mickey Rose, he had to be compelled to study Shakespeare and did

so with bad grace), but because of his reputation for selling gags to professional comics. Concerning the pseudonym he later adopted, accounts vary: his father states that it derives from his beloved baseball bat and his admiration for the clarinettist Woody Herman. Other people see in it the simple association of his college 'Midwood' with his first name 'Allan'; Woody himself insists the choice was totally arbitrary.

When he took the subway train at Flatbush and alighted in Manhattan, Woody found himself on the fertile territory of show-business. Between 57th Street, and Sammy's Bowery Follies, where his father worked as a waiter, there was spread the picturesque area which Woody was to evoke in *Broadway Danny Rose*, a concentration of jazz clubs, bars, delicatessens, drug stores and restaurants. It was the meeting place of agents and comics looking for engagements. Usually they all met late at night, in the famous Lindy's, comics sitting in the middle, according to Jack Rollins, agents on the left, musicians on the right.* Everyone flocked there to buy sketches and gags or to chat about the daily happenings in the 'Borscht Belt', the network of little hotels, family-run boarding houses and colonies of bungalows in the Catskills and Adirondacks, the stamping ground for the tribe of stand-up comics, Jewish for the most part. During the 1950s the Borscht Belt provided useful weekend engagements for singers and comic monologuists. Besides a breath of fresh air and an easily reachable clientele, a few weeks spread over several night-clubs in New Jersey, three-quarters of an hour's drive from New York, enabled them to refresh themselves financially and polish their acts for the dreamed-of engagement in the metropolitan night-clubs which were more or less under Mafia control and where bookmakers, gamblers and impresarios rubbed shoulders in a Damon Runyon atmosphere.

Many times in his own films (*Annie Hall*) and in those of other talents (*The Front*), Woody has evoked the feverish activity, galloping anxiety and cold sweat of the stand-up comic in front of an unattentive, talkative public packing the smoky night-clubs where he made his arduous start: sweaty palms, an inaudible microphone, unreliable acoustics, insalubrious dressing rooms were hardly kind to the comedy of this precocious learner, an on-the-spot retailer of some very loosely strung together stories. His shoulders hunched up, his body twisted around the microphone, his main problem lay in overcoming his self-consciousness – loosening up, yet not risking the audience's inattention.

Art D'Lugoff, owner of the Village Gate, remembers a kid, stiff and awkward with stage fright, lacking in presence, who looked for the exit when brought face to face with the public.

* See 'Woody Allen Starting Out', by Fred Ferretti, *New York Times*, 1984.

# WORD FEVER

an overdose of mah jong tiles', such a writer achieves, in a way accessible to popular audiences, the mastery of the great aphoristic authors, Forneret, Lichtenberg, La Rochefoucauld revised by Ducasse, while at the same time becoming part of the feverish imagination of a Benjamin Péret or a Tex Avery.

He creates images as unexpected as 'the gallows with a lightning conductor', 'the letter box in a graveyard', or 'the smallest pygmy in the world ' – perhaps without even being aware of these distant literary cousins and their esoteric influence.

Much fun has been had with his one-liners, those phrases which are the object of so much envy among writers in their workrooms and in the offices of publishers. But Woody employs certain tricks of speech which sound so well turned that no reply is possible: they invariably let him have the last word, which he can use in a cajoling or assertive manner. This consummate art of *cadence* permits him to give his inventiveness a rhythm, even in mid-phrase, and allows him control of what one could call the 'word blender', the better to deploy his effects.

'A lovable character wanders in and out, commenting wryly on the action and distributing hot rivets.'

'My mother lay in a coma for weeks. She was unable to do anything but sing "Granada" to an imaginary herring.'

'The Cartesian dictum "I think, therefore I am" might be better expressed, "Hey! There goes Edna with a saxophone".'

Woody has the nerve for literally anything. A few of his bolder statements:

'Dostoyevsky, if he could sing, would sound like Ray Charles.'

'If the Impressionists had been dentists . . .' (Woody has written a whole essay on this fascinating topic).

Witty remarks that permit no contradiction:

'He was tap-dancing on my wind-pipe.'

It's not a paradox to state that such delirious freedom in his use of words was essential if Woody was to express himself by means other than words – in a completely visual way, one that he could translate into his own particular art, giving him real power.

From the verbal to the visual, from the paravisual to the ultraverbal: such skill was to marshal word and image into a triumphant sort of 'Wedding March' to be joined in marriage at the altar of Woody's brilliant art.

This is how he did it.

An *agora* of raconteurs at the Carnegie Deli recalls his beginnings as a gag man. (*Broadway Danny Rose.*)

**Woody on stage:** painful beginnings (re-created in *Annie Hall*). In time, Woody found his mastery in groping for words, his artful control of the hesitation that parodies the Little Guy. His timing became a thing of wonder. *Following pages:* Improvising during the shooting of *Everything You Always Wanted to Know About Sex...* (a sequence cut from the film).

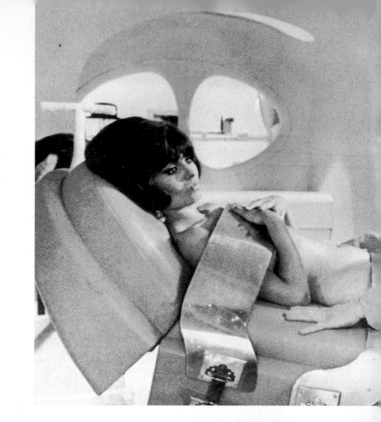

**Everything Woody admires in James Bond:** his power over (and fascination for) women, his impressive skill with firearms.
*Casino Royale*
Below: *Bananas*

THE JAMES BOND MODEL

From stage to screen, the ghost of Bogart – with his trench-coat – haunts and pursues Woody, even as he re-invents him.

*Play It Again, Sam* (above, right)
*Take the Money and Run* (above left and below)
*Bananas* (opposite)

THE BOGART MODEL

Homage to the masters of burlesque, also the masters of words.

W. C. Fields: *Take the Money and Run*
Groucho Marx: *Stardust Memories*

BURLESQUE

# ROMANCING

As we now know, it was the night-club comedian who provided the opportunity for the screen comic. Woody had reached his peak as a polished monologuist when 'The Midas of the Movies' (to give the producer Charles K. Feldman his outsize nickname) decided to turn the golden-tongued cabaret artist into the precious metal of the movies. Perhaps this little-known alchemist hoped to change what, in his eyes at least, was the common clay of comedy into negotiable currency. To a man as shamelessly in love with the box office as Feldman was, it would seem that Woody wasn't getting a reward commensurate to the effort he put into his act.

It was to the Blue Angel that Shirley MacLaine, on an impulse, had dragged the powerful producer. Feldman was secretly preparing a screwball comedy about an unrepentant ladies' man. He had got to know Warren Beatty, Shirley MacLaine's younger brother, who already had a reputation as a ladykiller of near mythical proportions. Feldman had a script, which didn't entirely satisfy him; more important, he had a title which he owed to Warren Beatty: the latter, while telephoning each new conquest, used to toss her an opening line that was extremely cute and, to his way of thinking, worked like magic: 'What's new, pussycat?'

The phrase had been rattling around inside Feldman's head. A former agent, he was in the habit of following the frenzied messages of his sixth sense. (He had represented the greatest names in Hollywood: Garbo, Dietrich, Gary Cooper, John Wayne, Richard Burton and had invented the forumla of the 'package deal', the ready-made film, which he was hoping to put to use again.) He knew he had a workable idea – a property as Hollywood calls it. It only remained to rewrite the scenario as many times as necessary and fine tune it till it really worked. And it was in quest of a writer that Feldman, accompanied by Shirley MacLaine and her infectious laugh, came to see Woody.

At the end of the act at the Blue Angel he had found his writer – and Shirley MacLaine's little brother was no longer in the running. A more prestigious name, that of Cary Grant, had become the favourite, although Grant didn't know it. As for Woody, Feldman, overcome by his talent, tucked him up inside a contract, going so far as to promise him a role in the film as a bonus, one that he could take his time over and write to please himself. It was current Hollywood practice to assure oneself of the close working relationship with any rather way-out scriptwriter by involving him in the production. At the eleventh hour – and this was a common occurrence – Woody's part was cut and he was put to work on another page of text. Thus it came about that the role of the psychiatrist was assigned to Peter Sellers, just as the Cary Grant part (previously promised to Warren Beatty) became Peter O'Toole's. 'That scene you mentioned to me,' Feldman said, 'we finally thought it would be better to share it between the two Peters.' And to console Woody, he promised him a role in *Casino Royale*, another of his projects.

Despite all these disappointments, Woody advanced from small fees to fabulous contracts, from the $1000 a week he was earning in night-clubs in 1963 to the $35,000 that Feldman gave him in 1965 to improvise a sort of script-in-progress. But it was small reward compared with the potential he possessed. Feldman later confessed he had been ready to pay $60,000. He could easily have afforded it, considering that *What's New, Pussycat?* cost $4 million and brought back $20 million, breaking all current records.

For his part, Woody grew familiar with the sophisticated world of tycoons, learned to work in movies, to travel at the expense of the production from Rome to Paris, London or Florence, acquiring an international veneer for his cultural outlook, which was already well established, by doing endless rewrites while often quarrelling with the great magnate.

At this time, he obtained a divorce from his first wife, Harlene Rosen, the inspiration for many much-relished jokes from married life in his stage act. (She was also the source of numerous stories which featured her as the unhappy victim and turned her private life into a national joke.) Woody later married a talented comedienne called Louise Lasser (who had tiny roles in a few of his early films). He installed himself in a luxury duplex at Park Avenue and 79th Street, with six rooms, a pool room, a jukebox, fruit machines, an electric organ and – finally – his dream: a collection of pictures that ranged from an Emil Nolde (won in a poker game) to the more voguish contemporary artists like Gloria Vanderbilt.

At the same time he settled down to being a regular contributor to magazines like *The New Yorker* and *The New Republic*. (He was to bring out three volumes of collected pieces: *Getting Even*, 1971; *Without Feathers*, 1974; and *Side Effects*, 1980.) He wrote stage plays (two inside three years: *Don't Drink the Water*, 1966, and *Play It Again, Sam*, 1969, without counting one-acters, *Death Knocks, God*, and *Death*.) And he played in ever more plushy night-clubs like the one in Caesar's Palace, Las Vegas (where he earned $35,000 a week) or the Royal Box, at the Americana Hotel, New York.

It's estimated that in 1966 he earned over $50,000 dollars out of *What's Up, Tiger Lily?* and *Casino Royale*, in which he made only a token appearance.

At college, Woody had put in sometimes fifteen hours a day without a break on his literary activities, and was reading the works of the great writers in a sort of uncontrollable frenzy.* Referring to his first play, he observed: 'Yesterday I noticed some scenes weren't moving quickly enough, so I tore out a page or two and noted how the action became faster.'

It was the same thirst for literary creation which was to lead him, in 1966, to write what was not exactly a film (since he had acquired one that had already been shot, a Japanese movie which aped, with an inadequate budget, the typical James Bond product of the time) but *a sound track* whose title *What's Up, Tiger Lily?* unashamedly echoed the one that had introduced him to the cinema, *What's New, Pussycat?* (Woody hated the title and tried to prevent the film's release). What

* In what order, it's impossible to tell, his choice being totally self-determined. Depending on the needs of the moment, he read the American classics, those of the Lost Generation of Fitzgerald and Hemingway, through O'Neill, Arthur Miller and the pillars of *The New Yorker*, especially Benchley, as well as Russian, German and Scandinavian authors.

# THE IMAGE

*What's New, Pussycat?*

Previous page: Double profile, dual woman. This reference to *Persona* (in which two symmetrical profiles form a single face seen from the front) becomes an almost Dali-like image of paranoia. Jessica Harper and Diane Keaton in *Love and Death*.

this amounted to was creating a film without actually shooting it. Using a plot which hardly adds up (finding the recipe for the best Chinese egg salad: a quest, it must be admitted, of only relative urgency), and surrounded by his friends of that period (Louise Lasser and his old schoolmate Mickey Rose), Woody devoted his energies to a marathon piece of improvisation comprising whip-crack ripostes, throw-aways, satirical commentaries and schoolboy humour ('Two Wongs don't make a white'), flippant sub-titles ('If you have been reading this instead of looking at the girl, then see your psychiatrist or go to a good eye doctor'), mismatched sounds and images... A linguistic collage, Foster Hirsch accurately called it.

Indeed, just as the surrealists used to join together ready-made film images from footage found on the second-hand stalls in the flea markets, simply for the fun of making them contrast with each other, so Woody found his images already on film and wrenched them out of context by inventing a new plot, cutting in musical excerpts from *The Lovin' Spoonful* as well as animated sequences: in short, a mish-mash calculated to inspire him to a frenzy of ad libs and flights of verbal fancy.

The same year saw Woody's first play, *Don't Drink the Water*, being staged on Broadway: he was its sternest critic, but obviously didn't see it the way others did since it drew a lot of laughs. Although a mediocre film was made of it in 1969 by the comedian Howard Morris, its theatrical virtues are remarkable.

Woody felt that *What's New, Pussycat?* had been ruined in production, and decided henceforth to only write for films if he could also direct. He felt the need to step into the arena – familiarize himself with this means of expression which he had lapped up enthusiastically and which was already shaping his outlook and making him venture on to a more airy plane than the claustrophobic cabaret stage.

Clearly, he intended his first attempt at film-making, *Take the Money and Run*, to be an apprentice piece, a beginner's work: 'I'm counting on a hundred per-cent improvement in the next film.' And indeed, in spite of his evident liking for parodying certain kinds of non-commercial cinema like the *March of Time*–style documentaries, the interviews and *reportages* in the *cinéma verité* manner of Leacock and the Maysles brothers, Woody still fell back on the techniques of the stand-up comic. The whole film had a voice-over commentary and the narrator didn't forgo any witticism, any crushing retort that echoed the director's previous career.

In it, the famous criminal Virgil Starkwell, whose physique automatically belies his terrifying reputation, is wanted in six states for robbery, armed hold-up and illegal possession of a wart. At his birth his parents baptized him Jonathan Ralph, after his mother. The witnesses to his early life speak directly to the camera and say their piece in turn like so many stand-ins for Woody Allen himself. The sketches follow each other with a constant emphasis on verbal wit, that familiar territory where Woody felt safe.

The best scene in the film, the hold-up, shows Virgil Starkwell (a name inspired by Charles Starkweather, the notorious public enemy of the 1960s) raiding a bank. He loses precious minutes over the language problem. Pushing an illegible note through to the teller, he then has to decipher it for the man: 'You are being covered by a gun.' THE TELLER: 'Me, I read "a gub".' – 'No, it's a "n" as in "gun".' 'Sorry, I see a "b".' (He calls a colleague.) 'Here, what do you make of this? "Place $50,000 in this bag. Act matural" mean?' – VIRGIL: 'No, natural", with an "N".'

The scene, which has begun on an essentially physical premise, continues on the level of verbal wit for several minutes, during which all the bank personnel (and even the clients) get involved in the discussion. Everyone is drowned by an exasperating melee of voices, a parody of the overlapping dialogue of sequences improvised by a would-be Cassavetes.

This raw beginner, however, was already enough of a perfectionist to have had some 'model films' screened for himself before shooting: *Blow-Up, Vivre pour vivre, Elvira Madigan, I Am a Fugitive from a Chain Gang.* He assimilated perfectly all these exemplars, like the writers whom he parodied in his articles, and reworked them until he had made a mockery of the cinema's claim to be a medium of truth and objectivity. By interpolating into his montage some venerable newsreels of Kaiser Wilhelm, supposedly the grandfather of Virgil (who fancies himself to be the German emperor), he was already discovering (some seventeen years ahead of *Zelig*) the shape not of *cinéma verité*, but of *cinéma mensonge*. Every protestation of truth is, in this case, accompanied by an intentionally distorted exaggeration of reality.

*Take the Money and Run* also paraphrases the whole of cinema. This work, in which he is still feeling his way, also contains references to the musical, the *film noir*, the sophisticated comedy. But Woody remains faithful in every way to the personality that he has created for himself of the rumpled hero – of the *schlemiel*. Brandishing a saw-toothed knife, he immediately loses its blade – which has been interpreted by one critic as an image of premature ejaculation! Other scenes depend on pure verbal drollery or are only made comic by a *bon mot*. Virgil, at the mercy of his gaolers, is condemned to 'three days in a cell with an insurance salesman'. 'My father,' says Virgil, 'was a soldier who, after thirty years' service, was catapulted to the rank of corporal.'

The film received a good critical reception. They viewed this film as an 'extended monologue'.

The same fondness for parody appeared three years later in *Bananas* (1971), in which Woody imitated "The Wide World of Sports," whose host, Howard Cosell, covers on live television the assassination of the president of a Latin American republic as if it were a sports event. This time, emboldened by his first experiment, Woody worked in conditions of real live television. He shot the entire assassination sequence in one day, spent with Howard Cosell in Puerto Rico. In a bare two hours he shot the president's death scene, then sent Cosell home by air at the end of the afternoon. He had decided to adopt an impromptu style of comedy: broad, fast, and uneven like the farces of Chaplin or the Marx Brothers – slapdash was the word he used.

One characteristic his growing technique had already acquired was – speed. *Bananas*, certainly, was shot very quickly, but in the manner in which, (so he said) S. J. Perelman wrote his scripts: 'I make one joke on the way to another while keeping a third one in the background.' Taking the risk of being accused of enlarging a simple cabaret sketch to the proportions of a feature film, Woody made the *bons mots* rain down: "I remember when I was a little boy I once stole a pornographic book that was printed in braille. And I used to rub the dirty parts." And: 'have you ever been to Denmark?' – 'Yes, I've been to the Vatican.' – 'But the Vatican is in Rome.' – 'They were doing so well that they opened a branch in Denmark!'

Fielding Mellish, the film's hero, is put on trial in his own country, in the course of which, drunk on his own rhetoric, he cross-examines himself and suffers not only a travesty of justice, but 'a travesty of a mockery of a sham of a mockery of a travesty of two mockeries of a sham'.

*Bananas* is a play on the phrase 'banana republic' and on the epithet 'bananas', meaning crazy enough to be locked up, as well as an implicit *hommage* to the familiar titles of the Marx Brothers' movies. (*Coconuts, Horsefeathers,* etc.), and had aspirations to be a topical film based on the way-out fringe of American opinion with which Woody, who is apolitical in his work, ranged himself when he described his work as 'coincidentally political'. It allowed direct reference to the trial of the Chicago Seven and a lampoon of the 'Castro ethic' – 'We lead the world in hernias,' affirms the fictitious dictator of San Marcos.

However, quick to sense the need to renew himself before anyone suggests it to him, Woody invents imagery that's striking enough not to need words. Fielding Mellish dreams that he is being carried on a cross through the streets of New York by a procession of flagellant monks. At a street corner an identical procession appears. The two processions then fight to claim possession of the only parking place. This literal 'cartoon', mocking the overloaded urban transport system, betokens a desire to counterpoint pages of dialogue by an occasional resort to the purely visual.

Woody was to go even further in the direction of the set piece with *Everything You Always Wanted to Know About Sex But Were Afraid to Ask* (1972) whose most famous sequences are pure action. Although his basic idea was satirical (a matter of making a film out of a bestseller: a manual written by a celebrated sexologist, Dr David Reuben, who claimed to have catalogued the whole spectrum of sexual habits) Woody gave free rein to his own sexual obsessions. A surrealist when it comes to classifying the unclassifiable, he disposes of 'statistics' in order to liberate uncontrolled erotic fantasy. In his galloping imagination a gigantic breast pursues him across a field before it's taken prisoner by a bra of the same dimensions. A spermatozoon dressed like a cosmonaut and played by Woody himself goes through the traumatic experience of being ejaculated alive out of a colossal penis that resembles a space rocket in a delicious take-off of the famous *Fantastic Voyage* through a human body which Richard Fleischer directed. Woody treats the most indelicate topics one after the other with a lively wit: Are transvestites homosexual? Why do some women have trouble reaching orgasm? What is sodomy? And so on . . .

Despite some comic embroideries of a cinematic kind or a few deliberately indecent sketches (a TV panel game on the lines of *What's My Perversion?*) or facetious anachronisms (in one medieval episode: 'I must think of something quickly, because before you know it the Renaissance will be here and we'll all be painting') the accent of interest remains on the funny visual effect: the terrifying splendour of the mammary fantasy which goes even further than Fellini, the Kubrick-like vertigo of the space station, or the innumerable work-force toiling away like galley slaves to free a stubborn spermatozoon.

Notwithstanding the mish-mash of topics, the film achieves an undeniable unity because it gives licence to the madcap eccentricity of the form.

It was the last sequence about the giant breast, a masterpiece of gargantuan suggestiveness and fidelity to Woody's feverish imagery that conveniently reflected an already very individual attitude to sex, which may have encouraged Woody to choose for his next subject *Sleeper* (1973) a prophetic view of the world worthy of H.G. Wells. The resemblance is nowhere stressed, yet the notion of a journey through Time (like the journey through the human body) of a human guinea pig put into a state of involuntary hibernation permits our auteur exactly the sort of para-scientific speculation with which to push his sense of the incongruous to the limit.

The futuristic adventures of Miles Monroe who is accidentally projected 200 years hence into a dehumanized future, as a consequence of what he calls a 'cosmic screw-up', gives Woody the chance to seek the technical perfection he desires. Not only does he give a believable shape to a technological and architectural fantasy, well articulated thanks to clever gadgetry and the utilization of some cunningly adapted 'pilot projects' (one recalls George Lucas using the pair of experimental subway trains in his first film *THX 1138*), but he also tries his hand at a classic burlesque turn in some of the action scenes like the unequal fight with a folding metal ladder, the grotesque imitation of a robot, etc. Woody at grips with some of the berserk machines is in the honourable tradition of *Modern Times*: but to Chaplin's forced-feeding machine, Woody obviously prefers an erotic piece of mechanism, the 'orgasmatron', whose mechanics are never demonstrated – the name alone supplies the joke. One laughs at the very notion of the sexually obssessed Woody having to wait until the year AD 2173 in order to find a machine which conveniently procures the desired orgasm for him without the obligatory foreplay and the appropriately named 'labour' of having to perform.*

Woody has frequently said that he finds all food funny and a source of comedy: in *Bananas*, a guerrilla army stops at the inn and orders 1000 grilled cheese sandwiches, 300 tuna fish and 200 bacon, lettuce and tomato sandwiches; in *Sleeper*, he's threatened by a jelly with a perverse life of its own.

Tempted back once more to the era of Mack Sennett, Woody avoids having to perform crazy chases, somersaults and pratfalls: instead, he mimes an individual taken out of the deep freeze who comes gropingly to life, clumsy and unsteady. He recalls Harry Langdon when he sees himself as a white-faced clown and slips on the banana skin that he has rehearsed well in advance, but which filmgoers feel he has put in place the minute he is satisfied with a tumble. Although his physical dexterity attains its highest pitch here, *Sleeper* seems to have satisfied a long-repressed liking for mime, a nostalgia for the silent cinema which for him is akin to the seductive myth of the past. In the year AD 2173, music is played on the clarinette by Woody himself and his usual orchestra, the Preservation Ball Jazz Band from Michael's Pub, a group in which he's stayed a faithful member right up to the present!

Bewildered like Miles Monroe in the twenty-second century, Woody the eternal outsider belongs to neither the tradition of slapstick (he has no training in acrobatics, dancing or balancing acts and wasn't a part of that era when players knew how to do everything: sing, tap-dance, ride a horse), nor to the tradition of Borscht Belt wisecracking out of which his ambition grew. So he is compelled to row his boat between these two seas and invent a wholy personal style of comedy – a well-blended fusion of the two extremes.

This period of striking imagery deployed in every possible way ended with Woody's most ambitious film (he has often

* A strange premonition: Miles Monroe, casting a retrospective glance at the past, discovers that a President called Nixon has apparently committed such a heinous crime that all records of it have been destroyed, like the tape which self-destructs on command. In other words, Woody 'foresees' not only Watergate, but Watergate's own Watergate.

called it his favourite). It is not only his sole attempt at large-scale spectacle, but also his most elaborately conceived and philosophical film. Its scale is suggested by its title, *Love and Death* (1975). I call it his most ambitious since it's the work in which the intellectual investment is richest: it's nearest, too, to the great high-quality movie spectaculars whose standards, at that time, were those of Dino De Laurentiis's international super-productions.

Perhaps one feels more comfortable associating Woody with his autobiographical films; but it is starting with this one that he gives the feeling he could undertake anything, seeking the most lavish creative resources yet becoming financially viable seven years before he won his Oscar.

I don't think it was out of respect for the title of Tolstoy's famous novel that *Love and Death* was re-titled *War and Love* (*Guerre et amour*) for the French public. French distributors no doubt felt that the word 'Death' in the title of a comedy risked being off-putting. What was rightly so interesting about the film was that it was the first comedy devoted to this serious subject – death, decease, the end of things. Woody Allen, that extravagant worrier about his own well-being, joined the ranks of the existentialist film-makers beside Sjostrom, Bergman, Lang and Delvaux. The appearance of Death, his scythe in his hand, in the middle of a satirical comedy, did not satisfy him, we can be sure. But Woody's preoccupation with the anguish of living, the fear of nothingness, is something rare enough in the history of comedy for one to dwell on it a moment. Buster Keaton was certainly haunted by thoughts of suicide and fought against an inimical destiny in every conceivable shape. But his was always a physical confrontation – against whirlwind, riot, ocean, Mafia, machinery, vehicles. His metaphysical limits are those of the man of action, his resilience is physical.

Woody Allen, on the other hand, needs words to express an intellectual form of humour. The idea of annihilation, the concepts of disease and infirmity, preoccupy him more than their outward appearances. He has also more of Hamlet about him than Buster although the latter may have been the first to parody, skull in hand, the neurotic resident of Elsinore. Buster does not detract from Woody who deliberately makes use of Dostoyevsky, Chekhov and Schopenhauer while aiming for the largest possible public – and reaching it, moreover, with greater and greater sureness. After all, we are dealing with a professional writer who has a history of innumerable published articles, scenarios, essays, stage plays.

But if he had to wait until his fifth production in order to get to grips with his favourite subject, the journey to the beyond, he had never stopped manoeuvring around it. Let me quote a couple of his celebrated *bons mots* for example: 'It's impossible to experience one's own death objectively and still carry a tune.' Or: 'I'm always asking myself if there's an after-life and if rents are controlled there. Can one get change for twenty dollars there?' In an interview given to *Newsweek* he confessed to having a serious vein in his make-up: 'There is something second-rate about comedy. Comedy just pokes at problems, rarely confronts them squarely. Drama is like a plate of meat and potatoes, comedy is rather the dessert, a bit like meringue.'

So why does one laugh so loudly at *Love and Death* and why, with its abundance of dialogue, is it, along with *Sleeper*, the most superbly visual of his films? It is because Woody is becoming more and more the all-round film-maker and because pure slapstick, an automatic return to basics, finds its place in it without straining for it. The soldier Grouchenko

*Love and Death*

41

undergoing training (one thinks of Raskolnikov in the regiment), the smirking advances of the man in uniform to the beautiful countess from one box to the other at the opera, the Battle of Borodino (as well filmed as King Vidor managed to do it in *War and Peace*, despite fifty times fewer resources) with Boris, inside a cannon, racing down the hillsides: it is all excellent silent cinema set to Prokofiev's music. Just as the dream of the coffins with the waiters is pure Scandinavian *onirisme* without one word of commentary – that is what remains first and foremost in one's memory.

Yet these are not the most original moments in the film. They often depend on crushing rejoinders like: 'Napoleon's invaded Russia!' – 'Why? Is he out of Courvoisier?' Or else false pleonasm like: 'My father owned a valuable piece of land.' accompanied by a shot of the father, a fragment of earth in his hand. The film's intellectual tone is tempered by deliberate anachronistic Americanisms: 'No kidding!' 'Oh, boy!' 'My mother, folks!'

One example of Woody's remarkable store of words and ideas: In order to warn the Russian Army about the dangers of syphilis, a little drama is staged in front of the soldiers in which, after making love, a pimple appears on the partner's lip. 'What did you think of the play?' a soldier asks Woody, who immediately delivers a review couched in the tone of *Time* magazine: 'It was weak. I was never interested although the part of the doctor was played with gusto and verve. And the girl had a delightful cameo role. A punkish satire of contemporary mores. A droll spoof . . . more the heart than the head.' 'Where schoolboy humour or sophomore wit is concerned, Woody was already the darling of the campus crowd, which guaranteed him quite a vast audience; but now he was swotted up like a course on Humour in Six Lessons, his context scrutinized, his intellectual zest submitted to analysis. He was also a subject for the cinephile as much as for the literary scholar. In *Love and Death* one comes across an allusion to Eisenstein's *Potemkin* as well as a composition from Bergman – the 'double profile' shot out of *Persona*.

Consequently, he is one of those movie talents whose original script has to be read, if only to get the full value of the dialogue. Giving every priority to the visual image, he whittles down the words before the shooting, pruning his thoughts and encapsulating them. Consider these pearls of wisdom from a conversation between Boris and Sonia in the eternal birch woods of the Russian autumn:

SONIA: Boris, look at this leaf, isn't it perfect. And this one, too. Yes, I definitely think this is the best of all possible worlds.
BORIS: It's certainly the most expensive.
SONIA: Isn't nature incredible?
BORIS: To me nature is . . . I don't know, spiders and bugs, and then big fish eating little fish, and the plants eating plants, and animals eating . . . It's like an enormous restaurant is the way I see it.

In spite of all the editing which gives the cinema of pure comedy its decisive rhythm, *Love and Death* remains a farce based on ideas, a satirical meditation on the thought processes themselves, a comedy of procrastination. The parallel with Chekhov is strengthened by the blue-stocking mumbo-jumbo:

SONIA: Immorality is subjective.
BORIS: Yes, but subjectivity is objective.

The literal illustration of a gag-line: 'My father owned a valuable piece of land.'

SONIA: Not in any rational scheme of perception.

BORIS: Perception is irrational, it implies the imminence.

SONIA: But the judgment of any system or *a priori* relation for phenomena exists in any rational or metaphysical or at least epistemological contradiction to an abstract and empirical concept such as being or to be, or to occur in the thing itself or of the thing itself.

All Woody's references to money, taxes or social security, appearing suddenly in this Dostoyevskian parody, don't diminish its intellectual impact – rather, the contrary.

The obsession with food here assumes an explicit formulation.

BORIS: Imagine your loved ones conquered by Napoleon and forced to live under French rule. Do you want them to eat all that rich food and those heavy sauces? Do you want them to have *soufflé* every meal and croissants?

A little later, the confrontation between Napoleon and Russia leads to a contest of chauvinist dishes: a 'Napoleon'* versus the 'boeuf Wellington'.

What one requires is a separate study of the fascination that culture possesses for American comics, from Stan Laurel to Jerry Lewis, from the self-taught to (dare one say it?) the self-declared intellectuals. Why this passion among slapstick clowns for Hamlet, Napoleon, Dr Jekyll, Camille? Why this continuous comparison between silly vaudeville sketches and the classics of literature, or even the best-sellers from Elinor Glyn to Margaret Mitchell? Why does the screen comic so frequently grapple with classical music, nuclear physics, the higher mathematics, if it's not through an attraction of opposites, a parody of knowledge through innocence?

Woody Allen represents the extreme development of this. He is the first well-read man (since Chaplin) to want to clap a jester's cap on his existential anxiety. Clowns make fun of their masters' infallibility: this learned fellow, condemned to be laughed at for his humble mien, can acquire social status only by becoming an artless genius, a teller of epic tales, a man of snap judgments. 'God is an under-achiever,' Woody decrees. Living proof of a divine cock-up which hasn't been reported to the Creator. *Love and Death*, whose theme is very similar to Chaplin's *The Great Dictator* and Jerry Lewis's *Which Way to the Front?*, is not the most egotistical of these three films. Chaplin and Lewis, men whose megalomania is bigger than their targets, preceded Woody with their mockery of political assassination, doubles, the power drive at its crudest and the *commedia dell' arte* at its most brutal: they fired off their Big Berthas, whereas Woody points the cannon out of *The Power and the Glory* at the heart of Tolstoy.

The higher form of 'nonsense', distilled into Woody's pithy remarks ('I feel an empty void' – 'We should divide the dead letters; do you want the vowels or the consonants?' – 'No, Russia is not my mother') is a late-entry in the Olympian Laugh-In; but no one before him had ever made crazy comedy out of plague, decomposition, suicide and the difficulty of 'being'. He handled ideas the way others handle cream pies.

In planning his next dramatic subject, Woody didn't concern himself with structural problems, or with production concepts or with receiving the Nobel Prize for Sartre-like gibes. No: he immersed himself in dissecting his own vocabulary. On re-reading him, it's astonishing to see the same words regularly recurring in the text: 'feathers', 'herring', 'midget' and 'butter'. There is something of Gide, Alain and Valéry in this Konigsberg, a name which has more in common with Austrian beer than with Ludwig II. I shall be the first to put my name down for his new volume of aphorisms or his future pillow books; for where the pithy phrase is concerned he surpasses all the leading practitioners of political wit. This Napoleon – this 'Little Napoleon', be it understood – is not yet short of Courvoisier. By dint of stretching, he is surely going to increase his stature; but at this stage, let us content ourselves with the perspective which makes *Love and Death* into a cross between Nietzsche's *Thoughts out of Season* (*Unzeitgemasse Betrachtungen*, a criticism of German cultural complacency), Alphonse Raabe's novel *L'Album d'un pessimiste* and Sterne's *Tristram Shandy*. And more cultural than that, one can not get!

---

* The cream-pastry that the rest of the world knows as a 'napoleon' is called in France a 'mille feuilles'.

**The use of slapstick:**
Slapstick, an inheritance from the golden age of Mack Sennett, enables all Woody's earliest films, even the wordiest, to rely on purely physical gags.

*Take the Money and Run*
*Love and Death* (below)

44

*Bananas*

Amidst the verbal gags of this film, one discerns the somewhat hectic efforts of the comedian to cope with very realistic material: a televised newscast which

has a sensational impact on Latin-American terrorists, public opinion and political assassination. Already Woody shows a taste for doctoring reality.
*Bananas*

**Illustration of a wisecrack** (opposite): chaingang escapees 'disguised as a giant charm bracelet.'

*Take the Money and Run*

**Subway, job, disaster:** the urban nightmare assumes the aspect of a Gethsamene. (Note Sylvester Stallone in the leather jacket.) *Below:* Two crucifixion processions have trouble finding a parking space: Bunuel would have loved this gag.

*Bananas*

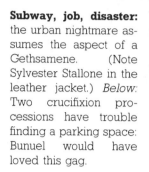

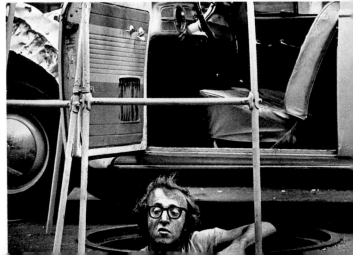

**The mad professor: too much knowledge:** Professor Alan Konig is dehumanised, the robot valet of the future but Woody retains his spectacles – and his individuality.
*Sleeper*

**Slapstick still holds sway:** with the help of a giant prop, Woody prepares for his inevitable fall on a banana skin.

*Sleeper*

Opposite: *Everything You Always Wanted to Know About Sex*

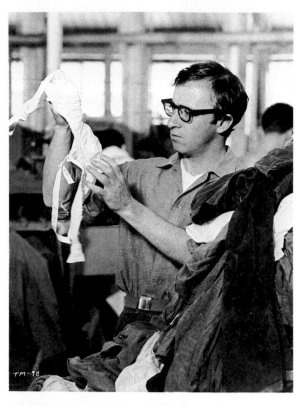

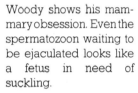

Woody shows his mammary obsession. Even the spermatozoon waiting to be ejaculated looks like a fetus in need of suckling.

*Everything You Always Wanted to Know About Sex* (Also on the previous pages)

From the left clockwise: *Take the Money and Run*

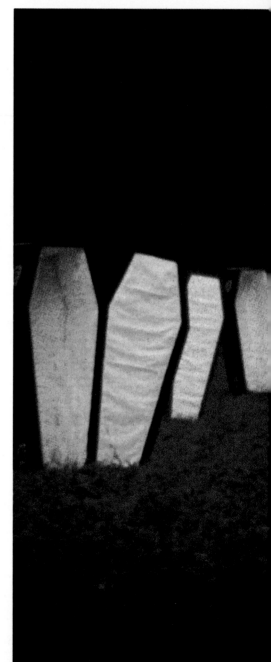

Woody's imagination is ever hallucinatory, surreal. This dream of funeral rites turning into a Viennese cafe waltz required fantastic and lavish organization.

*Previous pages:* Woody and Death: a celebrated twosome and a partnership destined to continue, since everything in it works to the advantage of both partners.

*Love and Death*

A Napoleonic super-production: to parody Tolstoy, Woody found himself for the first (and last) time directing armies on the march and heroic engagements: all the lavishness of King Vidor's *War and Peace* with infinitely more modest means and a far more economical production – yet nothing essential is missing.

The battlefield obser-
ver, turned into cannon-
fodder, is aimed at the
very heart of the story.

*Love and Death*

A calamity-prone duel-
list. With an epic taking
place all round him,
Woody fires in the air
and wounds himself by
the 'Law of Returns.'

*Love and Death*

Laughter
and culture **THE NAT**

70

'I don't know much about Classical music. For years I thought the 'Goldberg Variations' were something Mr. and Mrs. Goldberg tried on their wedding night.'

*Stardust Memories*

Generally speaking, culture has no place in screen comedy except *a posteriori* through the approach of criticism. One can write footnotes on the connections between Harold Lloyd and machinery, between Buster Keaton and Alphonse Raabe, between Harry Langdon and Watteau; but it's a safe bet that the first has never read Picabia, the second has never heard of *L'Album d'un pessimiste* and the third has never seen *Gilles*, Watteau's painting of a Barrault-like clown. Where the great laughter-makers are concerned, comedy possesses something natural and basic: it poses questions about one's vocation, it supposes (in addition to tremendous physical energy) an innate gift, especially a sort of inspired intuition similar to the gesture that an angler makes when casting a line, or the free brush-stroke of the Japanese calligrapher, or archery in the case of Zen mysticism, or the random splash in action painting. One can go hunting in packs for a gag, as was the fate of several armies of nameless hacks herded into their encampment at Santa Monica in Mack Sennett's day – which suggests very thorough physical experimentation and even scientific research of a certain order. But most of the time the great masters of comedy discovered the gag in a flash of illumination, like that evoked by the fateful electric light bulb in the cartoons. The 'idea', closer in nature to the work of Outcault or Wilhelm Busch than to Franz Masereel, impregnates thought and initiates action.*

Chaplin apart, the great jokers are rarely intellectuals. Groucho Marx was a con-man, with a glib tongue before he acquired his book-learning. Buster Keaton was the prophetic forerunner of a new kind of wit, but he understood nothing of its distant birth. He isn't to blame for the pain he has caused commentators and philosophers. He was a disciple of Beckett without having read him and he knew nothing of the resemblances between Kafka and himself. W.C. Fields constructed a literary luggage-locker for himself, filling it up with boxloads of books from the shops he came across while touring. But he was a reader with a core of Victorian sentiment who doted on Dickens – only to take the opposite view and create a reputation for himself as a misanthropic Scrooge. Jerry Lewis, for all his thumbing through dictionaries, reads very little and sporadically: he is the sole case of self-acquired pseudo-culture in the entire history of comedy who has achieved his own self-analysis unconsciously through his films and his

intuitive reaction to the American way of life. One day he'll succeed in turning himself into a veritable compendium of knowledge; even now, on TV talk shows, he can reduce political or scientific pundits to silence without cracking a single joke.

Woody Allen is thus the only comic of international renown who can be described as an intellectual; and far from wearing out his welcome, he has never ceased to entertain his public with shrewd but playful observations. He is the first to found a reputation on an instantaneous reaction to the great problems of our times and also to base his popularity on his adult personality – a sexually explicit one, too, despite the way he disparages this aspect of himself.

Let me enlarge on these four aspects.

From his very first films, Woody has always maintained his love affair with the masterpieces of cinema and literature. But he has done so with a kind of intellectual anxiety that can't refrain from quoting from his models and making the mass public privy to what one can call his 'wit-picking'. Accustomed to making people laugh at his own self-disparagement, his popularity sprang from the talent he possessed for approaching the average guy as if he were an intellectual or making him believe so. In fact, he knows very clearly which name to drop in order to provoke a risible reaction, which rarefied author he can parody at a stroke and, in particular, how to extract the laughter from cerebral by-play. Marshall McLuhan is probably none too well known in the lower depths of the Bronx or Des Moines, but the way in which Woody makes some idiot quote him in *Annie Hall* gives the average member of the public the feeling that they know him well enough to laugh when they see McLuhan emerge from behind a cinema poster and preside over the discussion. The important thing here is not drawing McLuhan into the act, but making fun of the habit of name-dropping among the snobbish intelligentsia. This kind of 'popularization', subliminal in nature, depends on Woody's fans, well versed in such matters, grasping all the nuances of the jargon, part-structuralist, part-Tom Wolfe, that is being endlessly mocked by Allan Stewart Konigsberg. But the astonishing thing is that with *Annie Hall*, which ranked very high on the American box-office returns, earning $25 million gross during the summer of 1977, Woody transcended this audience while creating his most intellectual film. What this suggests, therefore, is that he reached his largest audience without bowing to the perennial calculation of film distributors who always envisage an age group of twelve-year-olds. It can be said that Woody, in his own way, has made the American public more intelligent than it had ever been before.

* R.F. Outcault was the American cartoonist who created 'Buster Brown' and 'Happy Hooligan'; Wilhelm Busch, the German cartoonist, invented 'Max und Moritz' on whom 'The Katzenjammer Kids' (which I'll come to later) were based. Franz Masereel is the creator of the avant-garde film *L'Idée*.

# JRAL PHILOSOPHER

The fact that our hero had been a cabaret entertainer, a stand-up comic and a shameless monologuist didn't turn him into a chatterbox. We've observed how he acquired a real talent for dialogue and in *Annie Hall* a talent for deferring to others which acquits him of narcissism. But the origins of his art had accustomed him to commenting on political and social events in his own country. *Bananas* alluded to the Bay of Pigs, just as Woody's single show on television, *The Harvey Wallinger Story*, was based on Henry Kissinger. One is aware that Woody was very willing to take part in political rallies and that he campaigned for Adlai Stevenson and Mayor John Lindsay. And in conversation with Robert Mundy and Stephen Mamber he said that he found it very easy to make jokes about politics and that the gags which came to him from this source went out of date too quickly, or so he thought. But his sharp political awareness certainly helped Martin Ritt to interest him in *The Front*, a film that his volatile personality calmly appropriated without diminishing its significance.

But in *Annie Hall* he transcended snide political references, partisan hunts and the fashionable flavouring of the Mort Sahls and vintage Bob Hopes. He shows us by means of Alvy Singer, who is almost his alter ego, how the private life of a laughter-maker is nourished by politics. The long sequence in which Alvy and his first wife Allison discuss the Kennedy assassination and the Warren Report while in a clinch suggests a close link, to his way of thinking, between real events and one's most private behaviour. Alison isn't wrong when she says to him accusingly, 'You're using this conspiracy theory as an excuse to avoid having sex with me.'

One can take this exchange simply on the level of parody, laughing at them as one does at a character from La Bruyère (the liberal-minded intellectual who was incapable of achieving sexual liberation), but it is none the less true that such a sequence sounds as clear a note as any tirade on alienation in Antonioni's *La Notte* or Bergman's *Scenes from a Marriage*, a film which Woody has been drawn to many times. Despite the comic distance he maintains, he seems to be a person who takes politics seriously, getting worked up over an election, a strike or a scandal in the Senate. Among his favourite films is Ophüls' *The Sorrow and the Pity* about collaboration in France, several aspects of which preoccupy him: anti-semitism, of course, but also that of thought control, which he opposes with all his power as an affront to his civil rights, in a restaurant, say, or on the subway, perhaps consoling himself with a mischievous aphorism.

*Annie Hall* is also an important turning point in his work – his *7½* his mini-*L'Avventura*. This confessional work, heart-rending and funny at the same time, in which an introspective writer throws light on part of his private life with an overwhelming mixture of boldness and candour, represents a new frontier for the comic. Here he abandons, irrevocably, the image of himself as a *schlemiel*, a Yiddish term for a timidly inept little guy, which had no doubt grown too restrictive. One doesn't want to construct a controversial hierarchy where the great clowns are concerned – surely we've advanced beyond the stage when it was necessary to rank Chaplin and Keaton in order of merit, or, in present times, those contenders for the mass audience for comedy, Brooks and Allen – but one nevertheless has to propose a distinction here. With *Annie Hall*, it seems to me, Woody becomes the first great international comic who has advanced beyond the role of the simpleton, the innocent or the idiot, to portray himself as a whole man. Everyone else from Langdon to Danny Kaye, from

Chaplin to Jerry Lewis, from Stan Laurel to Gene Wilder, has incarnated a moonstruck hero, a puerile fellow who has scarcely put childish things behind him, a dreamer, an impulsive chap with no sense of consequence.

When they weren't playing this deliberately immature character, they embraced anarchy like the Marx Brothers or W.C. Fields, personifying heroes at odds with the world, out of joint with their times, occupying a Never-Never Land of their own devising. Chaplin, who enjoyed the reflective life of an intellectual, always took care to isolate 'Charlie' in the realm of allegory: the Little Fellow, the love-struck clown, the simple soul. And when he abandoned 'Charlie' it was for another symbolic figure, 'Verdoux', who was no longer Chaplin, but a fully-fledged propagandist with whom some people indignantly refused to see any kinship.

Woody Allen can co-habit with a woman without marrying her, break it off with her in recognizing his own shortcomings – eventually acknowledging her supremacy and remaining a loner, a loser, and all the while preserving intact his own comic charisma. Women, in what must have something of an acquired taste about it, have always been drawn to comics, even the least personable ones – Fatty Arbuckle, Chester Conklin, Larry Semon, Jimmy Durante, Ben Turpin, Joe E. Brown – and for better reasons, the ones with most sex appeal like Keaton, Lloyd, Al Saint John, Jerry Lewis or Danny Kaye, provided the latter awakened their protective maternal instinct or provided a comic equivalent to sexual satisfaction. Keaton represented tenderness at its most poetic, but his inamorata are always delightful scatterbrains or overweening Amazons and the romantic tradition of silent cinema culminated in a heroic embrace or a shot of two profiles pressing their lips together. Chaplin was an unforgettably bashful lover and he made a trademark out of that iconographic apotheosis of the two figures vanishing over the horizon, an undeniable symbol of fantasy. His fictional idylls were very far removed from his real love life, which no sooner seemed fulfilled than it began all over again. Even *Monsieur Verdoux* transposed into brutal symbolism the matrimonial and adulterous misadventures of the seducer that Chaplin really was. Jerry Lewis flirts with sexual reality only in the context of a counterpointing buddy-buddy relationship with a male.

Lewis's basic character, during its gradual evolution, remains that of the sentimental blunderer, the accident-prone lover or the unabashed dreamer: sexual satisfaction comes to him in symbolic form, like Dr Kelp's elixir of love or the vampire-like escapade with Mrs Cartilage.

Observe that Woody started in this category because it is an archetype of comedy, only to liberate himself from it little by little as he gained more control over directing. From the awkward emulation of Humphrey Bogart in *Play It Again, Sam* to the spermatozoon sequence in *Everything You Always Wanted to Know About Sex* right up to *Love and Death*, Woody wrung the laughs out of his would-be erotic disasters and their relationship to the larger stalemate of life. *Annie Hall* lets it be understood that everything is working out very well, thank you, and that he can sometimes be insatiable in those instances that he delicately refers to as 'playing hide the salami'.* He rocks the conventional comedy boat by saying such things as: 'You're exceptional in bed because you got – you get pleasure

* ALVY (on his love life): Hardly ever, maybe three times a week. – ANNIE: Constantly! I'd say three times a week. ALVY to Robin: I'm going to take another one in a series of cold showers.

72

Have you read Allen? The natural philosopher resembles Bernard ('Spinoza') Baruch in every feature.

in every part of your body when I touch you... Like the tip of your nose, and if I stroke your teeth or your kneecaps... you get excited.' No comic before him had spoken of menstruation, orgasm, sexual vibrators, aphrodisiacs; none had spoken about the breakdown of sexual relationships, the wrecking of a marriage, the friendly but sorrowful separation.

Of course I'm not making a qualitative comparison: a poetic metaphor can be more potent than the full-frontal approach to erotic anxieties, the explicit nature of which in Woody's case can perhaps be laid at the door of contemporary permissiveness. After all, who shall say in two hundred years' time, or in five minutes, which is the more up-to-date: Keaton, Fields, Lewis or Allen? I simply point out that Woody is, chronologically, the first comic to present us with topical and timely adult material, relevant to the everyday preoccupations of his generation.

Fortuitously perhaps, these innovations surface in what, from the viewpoint of visual inventiveness, is his most skilfully made film. The close-up shot of him delivering a monologue which opens the film is a means of exorcising the stand-up comedian. From that moment on, words cease to be paramount. The story conjures with time and narrative structure. The grown-up Woody sits at a school desk among the kids, like the hero of Carlos Saura's film *La Cousine Angelique*, while his childhood self kisses a girl who is revolted by this first sign of love: 'Ugh! He's kissed me!' But Woody pushes the conceit even further when the well-brought-up little pupils list what they'll be doing in the future: 'I'm into leather', 'I used to be a heroin addict. Now I'm a methadone addict', etc. Again when he goes back to childhood memories, he does a commentary on them for his friends like a museum guide.

During a love scene he uses sub-titles to expose his innermost thoughts; and he makes the mental distance of his beloved while he is holding her in his arms palpably visible through her ironic materializing as a spirit. He uses a split screen to contrast his own views with those of Annie or her family. He interrupts the story in order to interrogate passersby in the street, who respond with embarrassingly intimate details: 'We use a large vibrating egg,' says one passer-by.

This uninhibited film dialogue, uttered in tones of anxious frankness and disenchanted confidentiality, which is characteristic of Woody, disarms us through diverting us. We laugh because laughter is the natural element of this amphibian creature called Woody Allen. Yet it doesn't stop us from being touched by the frankness of the revelation and the mastery of his material. Note that if the film is entitled *Annie Hall* and not *Alvy Singer*, it's because Woody voluntarily assigns himself the 'bad' role, while, in a final dramatic stroke, giving the last word and the qualities he envies to his mistress. *Annie Hall* is, above all, a tribute to Diane Keaton, his first Galatea, who gave him everything, although they finally parted, and on whom he lavishes all he has to give by making this film about their relationship three years after it broke down.

It is on Diane Keaton that he bestows his favourite gift – loquaciousness. Annie gives vent to whole shoals of words without finishing a sentence – stammering, making noises, exploding with laughter, ending up putting herself out of action, pointing a finger at her forehead with the sound of an explosion. When Annie tells (very badly) a funny story (that isn't very funny, all things considered), the one about the guy who suffers from narcolepsy (or sleeping sickness) and dies while waiting for his Christmas turkey (they don't come sadder than that), Woody is exhibiting a form of humour that is absolutely not his style at all – therefore paying his respects to thought processes typical, one supposes, of Diane Keaton. Woody recounts hilarious happenings with an undertone of dread; Diane laughs till she cries over things that dismay her. His nature expresses incurable pessimism ('That was the most fun I've ever had without laughing,' Woody says to Annie after sexual intercourse). Diane is amused by anything and, according to *Time*'s reviewer, pulls up short in the middle of a sentence because she thinks she hears her tummy rumbling.

Faced with Diane's sense of humour, Woody can only come out with a feeble rejoinder ('Yeah, it's a great story . . . it really made my day,' he says about the death of the narcoleptic). But one feels he is lost in admiration when confronted by a life force that's so paradoxically the opposite of his own, one which he does all he can to place in the best setting the way Howard Hawks used to show off Carole Lombard's natural gifts. Surely Diane Keaton is the Carole Lombard of this later era. If for the first time one has the impression in this film of seeing Woody as he really is (or as he has decided to let himself be seen), it is surely because every man reveals his true nature when he meets his dream woman head on – a woman with whom Woody, in his own good time, also makes us fall uncon- strainedly in love. It's safe to say that after *Annie Hall* Woody turned into a social phenomenon whose private life became public property – the way that a collective myth can be appro- priated in intimate if invented detail. American *laissez faire* guarantees Woody's 'live as I want to' existence as well as his success, since everyone, handsome or plain, is assured of sexual happiness as if an income had been guaranteed them.

Writing, the act of putting pen to paper, is, as we have noted, Woody Allen's favourite activity – a cathartic process he's still not finished with even today. In his search for perfection he dreams of being able to throw away what he's written if he's not happy with it – and of being able also to throw away (although this is not so easy) any film that he can't remake from start to finish.

The more independent of their dialogue his films become the more visual they get and the stronger this desire grows. He expresses it with some precision at the start of *Manhattan* when, in the agonizing throes of *writing*, he cancels out his first appearance, reformulates and reconstructs his entrance into the narrative, like an East Side novelist with a Pulitzer prize in his sights obsessively reworking his first page so as to eliminate false starts:

IKE'S VOICE-OVER: Chapter One: He adored New York City. To him, it was a metaphor for the decay of contemporary culture . . . No, it's gonna be too preachy . . . Chapter One. He adored New York City . . .

This is the sort of liberty that truly *literary* artists take with the cinema: Sacha Guitry in his prologues, Billy Wilder and Joseph L. Mankiewicz in their asides and digressions. All of them have experienced the overwhelmingly narcissistic pleasure of writing as Gide once put it: 'I am writing *Paludes*' – a book about a writer who is writing a book called *Paludes*. Commercial and critical success, far from satisfying Woody's appetite, only occasioned him greater worry. A complex indi- vidual he certainly is! He envies J. D. Salinger for being able to enjoy the luxury of writing without publishing. 'But that demands an almost Oriental discipline, of which I'm incapable,' he adds.

At the same time he who lives by the pen dies by the pen every dawn. Unlike other comic auteurs, he is held to have no right to demonstrate scorn or show a lack of humour. Worse still, he is the victim of his own driving compulsion to do better, to overcome the dissenting opinions.

*Interiors*, as we shall see, may owe its origin to the perverse reaction to *Love and Death* of the New York critic John Simon: 'We could have gotten the same effect from laughing gas, sneezing powder or a mutual tickling session with a friendly prankster.' Such a molotov cocktail flung by one of the most influential of New York critics at the most accomplished of his comedies up to then – the same words could be applied with equal justice to any comic masterpiece if one suffered from an allergy, a migraine or simply a lack of humour – probably had a more persuasive effect on Woody than other similar rebuffs. He had to try, once at least, to put his genius to the test without its customary sharp blade, that's to say without making use of a single gag-line. One could be grateful to Simon if, contrary to what he intended, he really encouraged Woody to seek the serious attention of his critics by setting out on a journey through what some have solemnly called a corridor of mirrors. *Interiors* as we shall see, refined his talent for holding life up to mockery, the way that Charles Nodier does.* It is possible that creativity based on the steady observation of everyday life, as is the case with comics, feeds on criticism!

In the same way, what triggered the idea of *Manhattan* (1979) may have been the persistent view some people have held since *Annie Hall* – artistic appreciation is certainly chan- nelled through a narrow perceptiveness – about Woody Allen's attraction for those of the opposite sex. None the less, it's an attraction that's undeniable by anyone who has ever witnessed him trying to slip unnoticed among his public. A perfect example of this occurs in a sentence written by Andrew Sarris, the *Village Voice*'s pundit and author of what is generally thought of as the definitive work on the *auteur* theory by an American critic.

Andrew Sarris wrote, in 1977, with the lack of humour which it is very imprudent to deploy when one decides to criticize a humourist, 'The notion that Woody Allen could be a convincing lover is unbelievable in the cinema', and he added that he persisted in thinking that only those men who look like Robert Redford, Paul Newman, Jack Nicholson, Burt Reynolds or Warren Beatty could be appealing to women. Woody had good reason to wince at this scarcely credible opinion. To Mary Blume, who quoted it to him in *The International Herald Tribune*, he said: 'Sarris is wrong: he's a small-minded guy; it's a dumb thing to say. That kind of thinking went out years ago.' But, as *Reader's Digest* might put it, the theories of aerody- namics which deem the flight of the bumblebee to be impos- sible don't stop the bee flying – and, moreover, making honey. The stiff-necked analyst comes a daily cropper when faced with the simplest creative act. The total impression that a film makes expresses more than a police report on the private life of a great contemporary film-maker. And *Manhattan* is the most delightful riposte that Woody could have made to such preposterous objections.

For this film frees Woody for ever from the tired old plot of the immature comic. Not only does he show the extent of his accession to the state of adulthood, but he goes one better and writes amusingly in the second 'attempt' at an opening sequence:

* Charles Nodier, author of *Fantaisies du deriseur sensé*, a collection of short stories whose title (roughly *Fantasies of a Wise Fool*) could sum up the entire works of Woody.

IKE'S VOICE-OVER: Chapter One. He was as . . . tough and romantic as the city he loved. Behind his black-rimmed glasses was the coiled sexual power of a jungle cat. I love this.

In this charming and observant film he and his hero are one and the same. He plays a guy leading a life that's simultaneously rich, complicated, rewarding and baffling, who has to face up to divorce, multiple love affairs and an autumnal romance with a teenager. He plunges some characters who are as modern and cool as it's possible to be into an often insoluble predicament, a *La Ronde* of emotions in which Schnitzler would make Warhol redundant. He gets far closer to stripping bare his characters in this film than in *Interiors*, which clearly owes its power and depth to *Annie Hall*. The analysis of Woody's style of comedy, and where he fits into it, owes much to this cathartic episode.

He was correct when he remarked to me (see the later interview): 'I think that comedies can be improved if comics occasionally make a serious film.' Was not Chaplin at his very best after he made the two uncharacteristic but great polemical works of his career, *The Great Dictator* and *Monsieur Verdoux*? Did not his career go into decline after he had lent himself to the maudlin *Limelight*? Woody's voyage to Bergman-land freed him from a stubborn compulsion which had very likely been torturing him for a long time. In *Manhattan*, when Mary Wilke (Diane Keaton) shocks Isaac Davis by attacking Ingmar Bergman and when his friend Yale (Michael Murphy) intervenes, she stands her ground and says to Isaac: 'God, you're so the opposite! I mean, you write that absolutely fabulous television show. It's brilliantly funny and his view is so Scandinavian. It's bleak, my God! I mean, all that Kierkegaard, right? Real adolescent, you know, fashionable pessimism. I mean, the silence. God's silence. Okay, okay, okay, I mean, I loved it when I was at Radcliffe, but, I mean, all right, you outgrow it. You absolutely outgrow it.'

Overheard *en passant*, as the story is getting under way, this dialogue could be regarded simply as a means for Mary, the Philadelphia blue-stocking, to demonstrate her complete incompatibility with Isaac. But on re-reading it, one could ask oneself whether such a tirade, written by Woody with Diane Keaton in mind, isn't ultimately meant to be addressed to himself. After all, it's directed at him by someone with whom he had fallen madly in love not long before. And Woody, now apparently at one peak of his career, had perhaps freed himself from his compulsion to be taken absolutely seriously.

Certainly, Woody is here recognizable as his hesitant, nervous self. We see him smoking, because he believes the mere act of holding a cigarette renders him so incredibly handsome in the eyes of his young mistress; but this conceit doesn't stop him from saying coolly after a love session with a more experienced mistress: 'Mm, it's very relaxing . . . I'm in good shape . . . You were dynamite. Except I did get the feeling that, for about two seconds in there, you were faking a little bit . . . Not a lot. You were just overacting . . . You should leave everything to me. I'll make everything happen.'

Woody, to be sure, demonstrates how far the comic's trade provides a perfect therapy for the modern philosopher. We know that he hardly ever has to turn to psychoanalysis now – he who, for twenty-two years, at $50 a session, has himself contributed to the advance of Freudian studies.

Of course, Ike Davis has a shrink, whom he calls Dr Chomsky and who, he says, bosses him like a 'Mothers' Institute'. But he doesn't seem to have consulted him in a long while. On the other hand Mary Wilke, who is the great screwball figure in the film, the living proof of urban alienation in a cultural milieu, hangs on to her analyst, drives him to distraction and treats him with a kind of condescending intimacy. She calls him 'Donny' when he bombards her with telephone calls, rather than the other way round. One might think it's she who is treating him.

IKE: You don't get suspicious when your analyst calls you up at three in the morning and weeps into the telephone?
MARY: All right, so he's unorthodox. He's a highly qualified doctor.

Viewed from this angle, *Manhattan* works against the grain of the earlier film, in which poor Alvy Singer paid for Annie Hall's psychoanalyst, but simultaneously got himself into a mess with his own:

ALVY: You know . . . it's getting expensive . . . my analyst . . . for her analyst. She – she's making progress and I'm not making any progress. Her progress is defeating my progress.

This time there's no analysis going on in two places at the same time. Only Mary seems to rely on her analyst to sort out her contradictory compulsions, which, however, do very little to inhibit her. No doubt she consults him out of habit, or because it's the done thing. For she progresses from one lover to the next without major worries, except those that she feels obliged to inflict on other people.

MARY (to IKE): You're not going to psychoanalyse me. I pay a doctor for that.
IKE: He's done a great job on you, you know. Your – your self-esteem is like a notch below Kafka's.

Ike seems to adjust very well to this intimate if unorthodox relationship. Twice married (like Woody himself), he forms a sort of Living Theatre for the era of permissiveness. His first ex-wife, a teacher at an infants' school who is addicted to drugs, has become a disciple of the Moonies. His second left him to live, as she admits, with another woman. She has gone from one extreme to the other, from involuntary bisexuality to triumphant lesbianism. At the moment it's she who is bringing up their only son, a boy who bears the burden of two mothers. Ike calls them 'you guys' and expects his son to be wearing a skirt one day. With two sets of alimony to pay and two homes to visit, Ike finds the time to have a husbandly relationship with a nymphet and to set up home with the mistress of his buddy Yale, a married man. All of which appears complicated, except to Ike, who not only keeps his peace of mind, but reasons with one girl and analyses the other. Finally, Ike conducts his own analysis by confiding his thoughts to a tape recorder which, better than any practitioner, will clear his head, once he's got over his disappointment about the only person he truly loves.

Let's omit the innumerable twists and turns of this game of 'switch partners' . . . Ike falls into the very agreeable clutches of Mary. To close the circle, Ike has to fall in love with his new partner at the very moment she does the unexpected, makes it up with Yale and becomes his mistress again. Tracy the teenager decides to go off to England. The surprise is rough on Ike who moves heaven and earth – dashing across New

York a little like Keaton in *The Cameraman* – in order to locate the young girl. He finds her in the lobby of her apartment building. Beside himself with grief, he tries overcoming her objections, but proves his own worst enemy. Everything that he's told her in order to persuade her to leave him now boomerangs back on him. A touching scene and a cruel comedy: truly heart-breaking, as Salinger might have done it. The young girl suddenly seems endowed with serene wisdom, the older man appears a raw innocent shocked by the discovery that babies aren't found in the cabbage patch.

It's a memorable moment, which ends with a close-up of Woody, distracted, disheartened, with years of dashed hopes on his face: the picture of lost youth, of sudden and premature ageing and of experience ousted by innocence after a thirty-year fling. In its emotional power it recalls the celebrated last shot in *City Lights*. In it, Woody finally wins his spurs as an actor. Henceforth, one feels, he has a new dimension which equips him, if he should wish, to take leading roles in other people's films.

*Manhattan*'s achievement is to be found elsewhere than in its story. The acknowledged aim is to show the cultural dissolution of a modern metropolis regarded as an obstacle to rational living and moral order. This overshadows the hedonistic aspect, which is what most people take away with them, dazzled by the musical accompaniment from works by Gershwin and the elegance of the New York skyline filmed in black and white by Gordon Willis, the director of photography. Whilst paying tribute to Manhattan, Woody has composed a polemic that transcends the situation comedy in which his characters seem to be enmeshed by creating a pitiless fresco of a New York that is under the sway of drugs, pollution, crime, looting and Marshall McLuhan, at the mercy of the patronizing rich, of promoters, of snobs, of culture vultures and ingratiating entrepreneurs: a capital of go-as-you-please and do-as-you-like at every point of the compass, where the entertainments of the intelligentsia are a mixture of Feydeau's misunderstandings with Marguerite Duras's pompousness and a shouting match in a pizza parlour with dialogue by the illegitimate children of Saul Bellow and Susan Sontag. It shows Woody, two years after winning his Oscar (for *Annie Hall*), saturated to the point of satiety with a culture that he sees in risk of imminent extinction – exhausted by the series of relapses, rejections and distortions it has had to suffer in a town where Ike experiences in Mary Wilke all the positive and negative stimulation of Manhattan and, in Tracy's company, his liberation and hope.

With the rashness of a Don Quixote, Ike goes to some pains to overcome his weaknesses and small self-betrayals and to force himself to find the courage and take the painful decisions of daily life. Ever since he made *Bananas*, which seems light years away, Woody has demonstrated his political pragmatism, a hair's breadth from an almost basic lust to take on the enemy which, to his way of thinking, is the shrewdest course of action:

IKE: W-e-e-ell, a satirical piece in the *Times* is one thing, but bricks and baseball bats really gets to the point down there.

Besides expressing these deliberately uncivilized views, he never stops analysing society the way Molière did – though this is the Molière of *Don Juan* and *Le Misanthrope* as one of Beckett's peers might have reworked them. He knows how to turn a love scene into an observation on evolution the minute the couple enter the Hayden Planetarium in the film. And out of a confrontation between rivals, squabbling over some infringement of their territorial imperative, he can create a scene reminiscent of Yorick in which the protagonists fall to musing in a lecture theatre when faced with twenty centuries of human remains.

IKE (pointing to a skeleton): You know, some day we're gonna be like him. I mean, y-y-y-y-you know – well, he was probably one of the beautiful people. He was probably dancing and playing tennis and everything... You know, uh, it's very important to have some – to have some kind of personal integrity. Y-you know, I-ll – I'll be hanging in the classroom one day. And – and I wanna make sure when I – thin out that I'm w-w-well thought of.

Pascal's sense of the Infinite and Darwin's theory of evolution give a centuries-old resonance to the briefer apprehensions of New Yorkers over the threat to the environment and Future-Shock. Woody Allen surpasses Bergman in the sense that he knows how to clarify his thoughts – he who thinks only of his own condition! – so as to analyse the current dilemma without distractions. He can take a straight look at himself, with all the flaws and frailties of a child of his time, but using the dual perspective of the autodidact and the comedian which furnishes him with that overview of existence, self-centred yet at the same time prophetic, belonging to a resolute and self-declared moralist.

Woody Allen, the Natural Philosopher, gnaws on the bones of dying civilizations until there is nothing left but dust.

**Split-screen synchron-icity:** two people's analyses, Annie's and Alvy's, are observed simultaneously. Above: Alvy and Annie visit her past.

*Annie Hall*

The romance of Manhattan: the film's extraordinarily intimate feeling comes from the poetic feeling of the city. Audiences share completely the *tête-à-tête* of the two protagonists. Woody's film may be autobiographical: but he makes us feel it belongs to us, too. (*Continued on the following pages*)

**The universal 'shrink':**
Dr Woodrow Allenstein, analyst and exorciser of tortured intellectuals – and of himself.

*Manhattan*

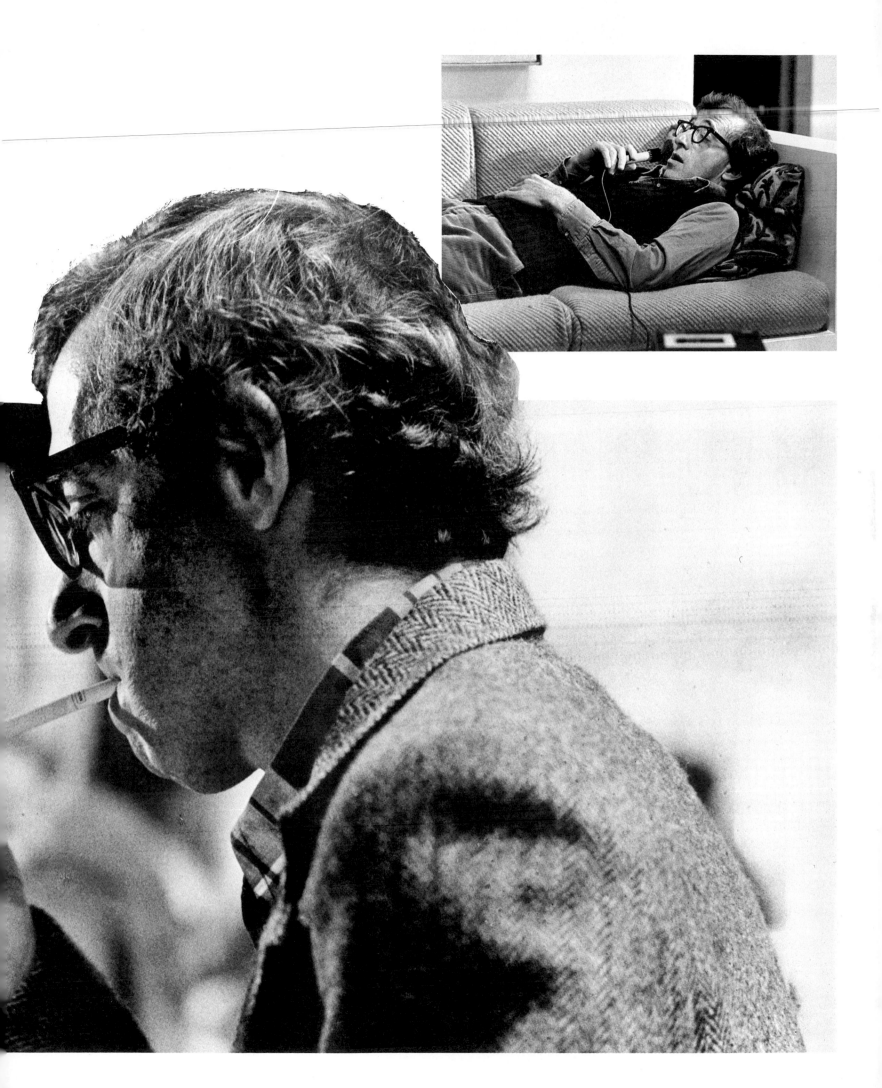

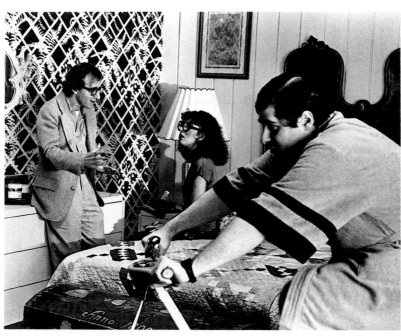

**The universal 'shrink'**
All his characters – the sister, the cook, the hippy, the French *fiancée* – all rely on Woody and depend on his intervention. At the same time he's confronting his own crisis and playing the lead in his own *Misanthrope*.

*Annie Hall Stardust Memories.*

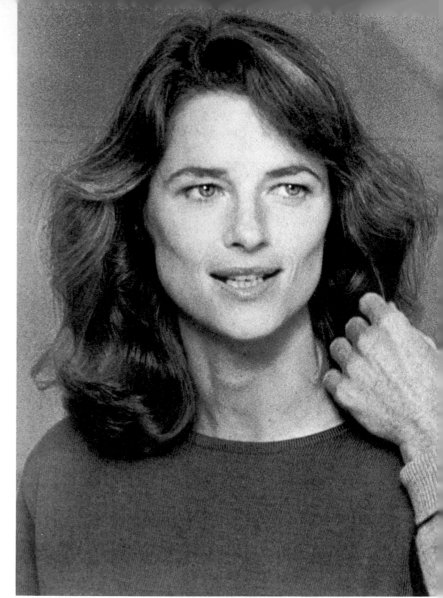

**Bergmanesque light
and shade:** a multiple-
image Charlotte Ramp-
ling develops before our
eyes into the full clarity
of Sandy's obsession.

*Stardust Memories*

Woody, photographed here by Ruth Orkin, measures up alongside the nobility of long ago, as painted by Gainsborough.

**A CU**

'I'm always chasing Rimbauds'.

**Dorothy Parker**

During the 1970s Woody Allen became a real cult figure. As far as his audience was concerned he could do anything, literally *anything*, so long as he kept them laughing continuously.

Yet he seemed doomed by his very success to remain a funny fellow and nothing more. He irritated and exasperated his admirers the moment he showed any ambition to extend himself beyond the sketch or the parody – even when he himself wrote it. *Annie Hall* and *Manhattan* were praised to the skies because they represented a triumphant 'double', two sides of a mini-fresco, but even more because Woody Allen and Diane Keaton, the new sensations of Big Apple, were playing characters allegedly based on themselves, demonstrating the lifestyles which rumour confidently attributed to the tenant of Fifth Avenue and his partner across the park. (As Woody has put it so neatly, gossip constitutes the New Pornography.) The real substance of these two works, for critics and public, remained the verbal genius and unfailing verve of Woody Allen.

But he still wanted to concentrate more profoundly on content ('I gotta find *meaning*') and in particular to address himself to the things that influenced him, which were generally European in origin. A jealous America plays an endless hide and seek game with culture. It wants to exalt its own culture and efface the diversity of its origins. Once Woody's films became celebrated and bankable, he was pigeonholed as the 'Ambassador of the East Side', 'Mr New York City' or 'Manhattan's Poet Laureate'. People didn't want to be reminded of the occasional warm words he had had for other cities like Paris, Boston or New Orleans, or his ferocious attacks on the lifestyle of Californians. Woody Allen, freeman of the metropolis, remained essentially a city type, a pure product of Broadway and Brooklyn.

Opinion remained cool when Woody announced his admiration for Bergman, Fellini or Shakespeare. It found this 'man of the world' posture unacceptable in a man who was as much a national landmark as the Statue of Liberty or the Brooklyn Bridge. And yet it is the right of every author who has paid his dues to refresh his talents in the company of those he has chosen as models and masters. All the works that illustrate Woody's intellectual debt to others seem to have had a curse laid on them: they came under a well-orchestrated barrage of criticism. Yet *Interiors, Stardust Memories* and *A Midsummer Night's Sex Comedy* are films illuminated by their own inner genius, shimmering reflections of uniqueness, multi-hued works which can unhesitatingly be termed Allen's *oeuvre*.

*Interiors* (1978), made between *Annie Hall* and *Manhattan*, is Woody Allen's first revolt against his own method of creativity, and we can be sure (or hope) that he'll stage many more. In a career that's already substantial, self-assured and bankable (his films have usually cost less than they bring back,

which gives him credibility in the eyes of his backers) this film represents a rash, almost insane act. That, moreover, is how it was received.

To make a film without a single wisecrack was, for a comic, as brutal an act of defiance as Chaplin's say, when, at the peak of his comic reputation, he abandoned the four-reelers* to make a melodrama like *A Woman of Paris* and escape from the fetishistic character of 'Charlie'. Does one need to be reminded that in spite of the unique position Chaplin held in the cinema industry of that time, he paid very dearly for his boldness and was pilloried (on political and moral pretexts) by contemporary public opinion?

Woody Allen, enjoying the relative luck to be an artist in a somewhat more sophisticated era of show-business, might have been attacked solely on grounds of principle. But one has to record that this first experiment directly inspired by a foreign culture was received with ear-splitting hostility.

Had Woody not been cast in the (admittedly still precarious) role of a beloved comic, adopted by everyone who claimed him as their ambassador of good-will, while wishing to keep him 'in his place', or if *Interiors* had come, for example, from an independent actor-producer like Robert Redford (the maker of a comparably ambitious venture, *Ordinary People*), then it might have been seen for what it is – an intense and austere film, a study of manners intended for a serious-minded and adult public which expected a film to provide something more than the rib-tickling that John Simon complained about when he disparaged *Love and Death*.

The intellectual and international ambitions behind *Interiors* suggest that Woody Allen is staging Chekhov's *Three Sisters* as it might have been reworked by Strindberg or O'Neill, engraved by Munch, painted by Nolde and imbued with music (for the inward ear) by Mahler. This flood of references isn't gratuitous: I hope to justify them in due course.

The film illustrates the crisis touched off by Eve, the mother in an artistic family, who shapes her personal life like the design for a piece of abstract pottery and discards all the bright colours from her basic design. (Her little interior is entirely picked out in touches of beige, grey or pastel). The crisis is resolved within the setting by the dominant notes of the tonality.

Eve has shaped her life like a collector's piece: she goes to the length of arranging an attempted suicide as if it were a still-life. And she has alienated her husband Arthur, a man traumatized by the Ice Palace of her creation: this is the initial trigger of the whole drama, the moment when the universe of an apparently well-balanced family totters and falls apart. To this extent one can regard the work itself as an observation

* Four-reelers: silent films in four reels, halfway between shorts and features and the standard format for comedy of that era.

# TURAL CHAMELEON

In this shot, Woody sees himself as Fred Astaire, in a dream of suavity and sophistication which anticipates the inclusion of *Top Hat* at the end of *The Purple Rose of Cairo*. Right: Jazz Heaven, the musical and womb-like dream, a milky way of desire for completeness.

*Stardust Memories*

on the possible conflict between form and content in a life constructed by purely external criteria – and from which *interior* existence has been excluded. The three sisters, Joey, Renata and Flynn, have been reared by their mother in a cradle of creativity which has compelled each of them to define herself according to her mastery of the art (or the man) she has elected to make her own: poetry, drama, the novel or politics.

The drama is objectively suggested by the tonal qualities of the picture, the composition in which the principal players are often partially cut from the frame and the texture of lighting and brightness. For once, the drama isn't simply verbal. Not only does the screenplay deliberately forgo all easy entertainment (to the annoyance of some people), but it also tries to be objective, ordinary even, without the least 'effect' or authorial touch, or even the boisterous, demonstrative situations of the theatrical antecedents already mentioned. Woody has here been sparing with words, in order to give every chance to the visual image; his references are thus entirely painterly ones: the grouping of characters, their attitudes expressive of their relative importance, the *clair obscur* lighting which irradiates their encounters and owes its inspiration to Edvard Munch. The colours have the freshness, the luminosity of the watercolours of Emil Nolde (a painter admired by Woody, who owns one of his works). The way the women stroll along the seashore is clearly Expressionist. And the pleasure one derives from looking at the film (once one has decided not to listen to it, since the *bon mot* never strikes the ear cocked for it) is worth the price that Woody paid to refresh his public's sense of anticipation.

Much as some people may wish to, one can't condemn this film as pretentious or élitist. Its very argument is based on just the opposite premise. Delivering judgment in his own fashion on the intellectuals he puts on the screen, Woody informs us that the artist, far from being a privileged creature, is someone on whom fate has perhaps unjustly heaped its blessings. (He himself has called some of his most lauded comedies 'overpraised'.) The artist isn't turned into either a prophet or a philosopher under the influence of his endowments: sometimes he is more inhibited, more limited in his way of looking at things, than a non-artist whose 'gift' derives from a direct acquaintance with life.* This is a populist view of art, a democratic concept, and in Woody's case free from all attitudinizing. It bears out, on the contrary, the idea that's prevalent in a number of his films, according to which everyone can be loved, be attractive to women, make a success of life and create his own cultural sensibility, an intellectual life of very high quality.

In *Interiors* the sole positive character endowed with a real joy for living is actually Pearl, the wife chosen by Arthur (and the antithesis of Eve) in order to restore some warmth to his worn-out body. Pearl is a sharp-tongued, earthy woman full of practical advice and simple tastes, whom Woody dresses in red – a device that no film critic misses, nor, doubtless, any filmgoer.

Joey, the only one of the three sisters not to have any

* In December 1978 Woody told Yvonne Baby of *Le Monde*: 'I live in a world that worships the artist and I have always had the impression that he was overvalued. Usually, it's believed that the artist uncovers the truth, that he knows the secrets of the universe, and has been born with a magic gift. Any ordinary person devoid of the divine spark, any non-intellectual who can approach other human beings in simple faith, gets closer than the artist to the meaning of life.'

particular talent (from the lack of which she suffers at the start), and who isn't motivated by any sense of vocation, is the sole person in the story with whom Woody feels any affinity. No doubt because she is the only one who accepts the need for change, the need to evolve: she is quite prepared to come to terms with Pearl, to accept her influence. She effaces herself behind Renata, whose outspokenness she admires. (And here Woody provides Diane Keaton with a mouthpiece role: 'She speaks for me, she articulates my own anxieties.') With no thought of her future, Joey wants to be a blank page, an open book. Through her, Woody informs us that art cannot flourish in isolation, hidden away from humanity. Just as he refuses to cut himself off from life, he has a need to measure himself against the great artists – Bergman on this occasion, other ones tomorrow – and to furnish himself with a standard of comparison, something he has lacked hitherto because of his particularized and way-out form of art.

This obsession isn't intellectual snobbery or ludicrous pretentiousness, still less a 'Pagliacci Complex' or a 'surrender to the enemy', as some people have said, referring to betrayal and even self-inflicted injury (as if, paradoxically, to be serious is to be opposed to laughter). It is based on his determined claim to be considered an artist. Using the privilege of foresight, we can say that Woody has never reneged on his intentions, never disavowed this experiment, nor the ones following it, even though the extent of the risk became evident only after he had taken it. Confirming Woody's first fears, *Interiors* was not box office, but it got a welcome in Europe, where his foray into this new genre wasn't made a matter of reproach. (All Woody's films since *Annie Hall*, including the comedies, have always done better in Europe than in the United States.)

Without provoking the same outcry, *Stardust Memories* (1980), an essay on the Seventh Art (i.e. the cinema), suffered an overkill of critical interpretation and literal analysis. One needn't stress that the film-maker Sandy Bates represents Woody Allen, speaks for him, or proclaims the manifesto of a comic artist in transition, in order to affirm that *Stardust Memories*, one of his most important works, represents the beginning of his farewell to autobiography and the start of his true works of fiction – works that, in his case, are more productive of real artistic progress.

Sandy Bates, a film-maker in his forties who is suffering from mid-life crisis, dreams about his earlier life, his moments of happiness, his childhood ambitions and his own films – all in a way that throws chronological sequence to the winds. Out flows a random stream of all his haunting memories, obsessions, and ambitions. We recognize both Woody Allen and his opposite number – the person he refuses to become and the one that other people would like him to be. He is the director–victim: a status he once sought and which now overwhelms him, a God-like figure forever engaged in reshaping his past (a typical preoccupation at such a crossroads). Our hero, no doubt like Fellini and Bergman before him, submits to surprised self-scrutiny, as if facing a blank sheet of paper, because he is too cautious to let himself be viewed objectively and against his will.

Sandy Bates *is* Woody Allen because his wit – whatever one's opinion of it – sparkles more brightly than ever with verbal quips and because the visual impression of his world has never appeared so rich and full of virtuoso sequences: tracking shots followed by the characters in long-shot or depth of focus, all inter-cut with simulated interviews, invented flashbacks, surreal fantasies, riotous crowd scenes that he sets amid the symbolic decor of an immense pantheon. At the same time Bates, in the shape of his *alter ego*, is summoned to a health resort in New Jersey to attend a retrospective of his imaginary films: bizarre *avant garde* parodies, musical interludes in which he sees himself as a music-hall star, cosmic visions of the Creation in which Bates, ironically, assigns himself the role of Zeus. One of his fans says to him, 'You're a master of despair' and another adds, 'Such a touch of Kafka' – a monstrous slander, blatantly implausible, though some critics have made it into a shibboleth. His producers, insist on re-editing his films (Woody's own producers wouldn't have had the power to do so). His manager harasses him with his reproaches: 'Human suffering doesn't sell tickets in Kansas City.' But overcome by the recent death of a friend struck down by a mystery illness, amyotrophic lateral sclerosis, he refuses to make any more comedies. (Woody has since made several.) 'I don't want to make funny movies any more,' he says, 'I – I look around the world, and all I see is human suffering ... Hey, did-did anybody read on the front page of the *Times* that matter is decaying? Am I the only one that saw that? The universe is gradually breaking down.'

At this point one has to ask oneself who is panicking: men of science stung by jokes about Frankenstein, PR men whose insomnia is guaranteed by the Constitution, or press pundits who missed the irony? The wonderful thing about Woody Allen is precisely the fact that he makes us amused at the very reasons why we have to fear the future, that he is at his best in the day-to-day context of unspeakable terror. As Sandy Bates puts it so well: 'We, you know, we live in a – a society that puts a big value on jokes, you know? If you think of it this was – (*clearing his throat*) if I had been an Apache Indian, those guys didn't need comedians at all, right? So I'd be out of work.' So Woody Allen – and everyone loves him for it – pours scorn on absolutely everything – permits himself to poke fun at anything at all, including disease, disability or death. To one of his friends who confides in him, 'Mom's blind in one eye ... deaf in one ear,' he replies, 'Oh, I hope the same side of her head, right? Because that's important, so she's even.' And, in a supreme piece of impertinence for a Jew, he commits himself to the following terrible verdict: 'I was a lucky bum. If I – if I was not born in Booklyn, if I had been born in Poland, or Berlin, I'd be a lampshade today, right?' Woody suffers, to be sure: perhaps from his generation's misanthropy; but like everything else that falls from his lips, this misanthropy is exaggerated, burlesqued and – why not? – blasphemous. To all those who were recently roaring with laughter, and now feel offended, Woody could say, paraphrasing the famous retort of a cameraman to an old actress who was complaining about how she looked, 'Madame, it's all my fault: it's I who am ten years older.'

Everything incites him to make heartless, irresistibly outrageous jests. He draws on the bible, the Jewish play entitled *The Dybbuk*, psychoanalysis, Ingmar Bergman (in a series of superb close-ups of Charlotte Rampling's face which recall those in *Persona*) and Fellini from whom he coolly borrows a religious-like procession, a series of photogenic monstrosities in the direct line of descent from Diane Arbus, Weegee and Helmut Newton. But this isn't the influence of other people, or plagiarism; it's one more example of his satirical borrowing in the manner of his parodies of Antonioni, Terence Fisher and Richard Fleischer. In one of the many interview sequences which are scattered throughout the film, and which Woody monopolizes, as if pleading to be forgiven his early days as a stand-up comic, one festival-goer asks his friend Tony Roberts about the origin of a reference to the Vincent Price horror movie *The House of Wax*. Roberts replies: 'An *hommage*? Not exactly. We just stole the idea outright.' Woody has certainly stolen from Fellini the notion of showing a film-maker who, having reached a certain age, has begun questioning himself about his art. But this film isn't at all Felliniesque. It bears the most recognizable mark of the Allen-esque wit.

This tiny, stammering, myopic man, plagued by a pigeon with a swastika under its wing, by hordes of admirers, whose doctor apologizes for having prescribed a hair tonic that causes cancer, and who, dressed as Superman, tries in vain to take to the skies: he bears all the stigmata of a sense of humour riddled with smiling hopelessness, comic consternation and stunned hilarity. If Sandy Bates were not Woody Allen, then the film itself couldn't have been conceived and executed by anyone else. Nothing that happens in it is autobiographical, except perhaps the childhood memories that are conjured up – Woody was a clever illusionist from an early age – but Allen's universe of calamity and hilarity is re-created almost unchanged.

The image of the cinema that he has created – his own kind of cinema – is neither populist nor imbued with foreign exoticism. It is never used for caricature, never springs from human catastrophe except in the most playful way. Even for the leading characters who wend their way through it, it remains touched by infinite sympathy. It is a sardonic, ever shifting vision, a rather metaphysical one. Woody Allen views the world of cinema, with its symposiums and its open discussions and its denizens of the *cinémathèques*, as a limitless extension of all his own frustrations, but also as a no-man's-land of the intellect, a rather Freudian underworld of myth which can be a blessed land of catharsis. As one of his fans says to him, 'It's like we're all characters in some film being watched in God's private screening room.' And when Sandy Bates encounters an extraterrestrial, this incorporeal but sharp-tongued entity behaves like a critic who prefers his 'early funny films', pries into his private life, ticks him off, comments on his choice of girlfriends ('What are you,' Sandy asks, 'my rabbi?') and exhorts him to save humanity by telling funnier jokes, then no doubt Woody is reprimanding himself indirectly. But he is also addressing himself to his critics, as if they had turned into Jewish mothers: stern, possessive, intent on keeping him up to scratch, refusing to countenance his change of hairstyle, his women or his job, embarrassing him with his baby's drinking-mug and requiring him to keep 'making sandcastles' for their benefit only.

Woody Allen, a modern movie-maker if ever there was one, has certainly acquired wide-ranging freeedom where the choice of material is concerned. He skilfully steers his way through the twists and turns of the story, endlessly passing from reality to fantasy, from what's suggested to what's explicit. More and more frequently he substitutes an *image*, an elaborate episode, for an *idea*, as in the sequence where Sydney Finkelstein's hostility, manifesting itself in the shape of a fierce gorilla, is seen being hunted down by posses of incompetent policemen. Halfway through the film Sandy Bates lets himself be killed by a gunshot from a rather too jealous fan and receives a posthumous acting prize, which doesn't stop him holding an impromptu press conference.

Nevertheless, *Stardust Memories* proceeds in the presence of the 'deceased' who, as an innocent creator, presides over

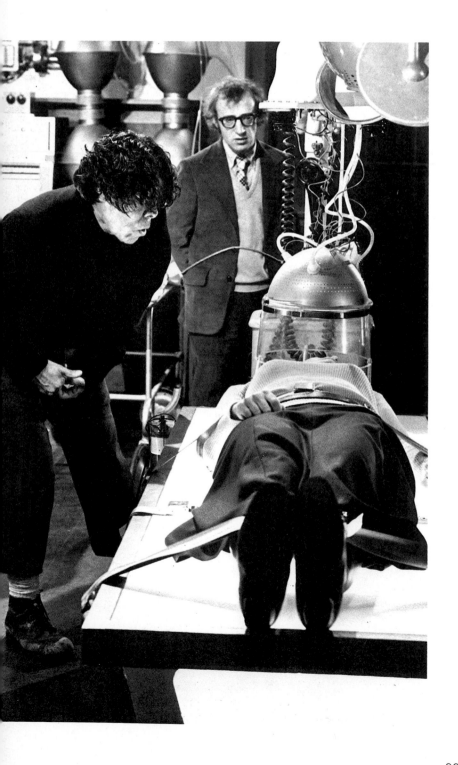

**Speculations on Frankenstein.** The myth of creation, as a cherished dream or a repressed fear, is shared by Allen as well as by his friend Mel Brooks (but what is pure parody in Brooks's case becomes simple metaphor in Woody's).
Top: *Young Frankenstein*
Left: *Sleeper*
Right: *Stardust Memories*

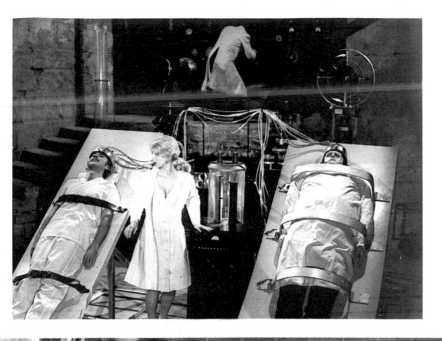

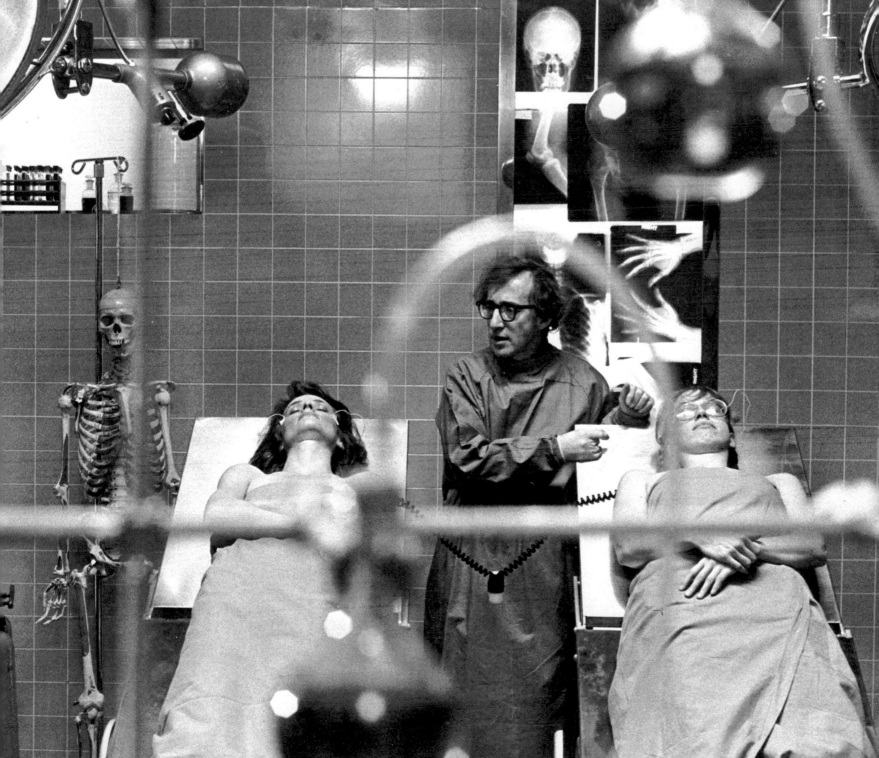

*Stardust Memories*

real life, master of his material and sometimes having no compunction about cutting it – the blank screen apparently testifying to a casual hand. The keynote of the film, when all is said and done, is the alert yet affectionate charm attaching to a man who is passionate about women and can extend a moment of happiness into a burgeoning eternity, like his evocation of a sad and wistful breakfast for two punctuated by a Louis Armstrong song – *that* is *Stardust* precisely! The film is set within a cinema and the audience files out arguing over it. Woody sits on alone, in front of his empty screen, seemingly lingering on in his dream of creation, an Adam, as it were, fascinated by Eden on a day of rest.

The elegiac tone of this sort of humour is also that of the latest Woody Allen film to serve as a votive offering to his muse: *A Midsummer Night's Sex Comedy* (1982), this time dedicated to Shakespeare via Mendelssohn. *A Midsummer Night's Dream* serves as the basic inspiration, though not the only one, and the film evokes the feeling of one made by D.W. Griffith with a countryside setting, modulated by reference to the Primitives of American cinema, like Stuart Blackton, the pioneer founder of Vitagraph, or, at the other extreme, the early animator Winsor McKay, creator of *Little Nemo*.

It's a conception that proceeds by allusive and eliptical means. A period film, about a weekend in New Jersey in 1900, it was shot in ravishing colour; and the out-of-town intellectuals, in spite of their very anachronistic dress and manners, conduct themselves like contemporary men and women of the world whose libidinous natures come to full flower in a rupestral rhapsody where hares and fireflies scurry and flit about, indifferent to the scientific discoveries of the most original kind that are being made. Youthful freethinkers and sententious greybeards are locked in vigorous rivalry in this pastoral setting along with comely tarts from Coney Island.

Shakespeare, seen from a Fifth Avenue penthouse, certainly; but from which Woody extracts a profoundly harmonious relationship with nature, a rhythm which, in the luxuriant bosom of summer, governs the psychic pulse as well as the physical passion.

Leopold, played by José Ferrer, is an ageing professor of political philosophy such as Gunnar Bjornstrand used to play twenty years ago in the light-hearted entertainments of Bergman, notably *Smiles of a Summer Night*. And Tony Roberts, in the part of Maxwell, looks a little like another Bergman favourite, Erland Josephson, in a straw hat. Woody appears less interested in reproducing the substance of Shakespeare's work – the spells of an enchanter which seduce the humans into losing their wits – than illustrating with joyfulness and frivolity a lovers' game of hide and seek very much to the taste of the times. Blending together Merlin, Caliban and Bottom, Woody plays a small-time inventor who might be from the Concours Lepine, the Paris congress of inventors, who has perfected a vegetable peeler, a Cupid-like autogyro and a magic sphere for picking up psychic vibrations. This fellow, whom one first takes to be unredeemably bourgeois, stumbles into the playful revelry of will-'o-the-wisp-infested woods and feasts his senses on the flux of flora and fauna in an unanticipated release of lyrical feeling. A pure exercise in style? Probably not: Woody succumbs to the enchantments of the countryside like a repentant misanthrope discovering the joys of dawdling *à la Rousseau*, but especially, it would seem, like a born painter.

One is reminded less of the masques and divertissements of Elizabethan tradition than of the mischievous conversation pieces of Fragonard and Watteau. Woody evokes the bucolic creations of illustrators like Arthur Rackham, Edmund Dulac or Richard Dadd, as well as those of the English decorative artists, all of them blended into the American countryside and absorbed into the swarming mass of nature as seen by the early Impressionists (Manet rather than Monet). Mia Farrow seems to have escaped from the canvases of a Rossetti or a Millais, brightening the undergrowth with her long, ringleted hair which, by abandoning her boyish style of other years, turns this blonde elf who had radiated an androgynous look for far too long into a womanly enchantress and endows her with a magic that needs no philtres to work marvels.

Some critics have made reference to Jean Renoir's *Le Déjeuner sur l'herbe*; and indeed we're concerned in this case with a *partie de campagne* at which the handsome, town-bred gents become involved with seamstresses and other menials in order to allow a time-honoured paganism to flow through them.

All these emotions are blended together: Woody has clearly no conscience about revealing all his sources, since they only recharge his creative batteries and keep him from becoming too narcissistic. Generally speaking, it's about a creative artist contriving to have an affair with every possible source of inspiration, classical as well as contemporary. Notice that, in all these experiments, Woody never lapses into empty imitation – his source of inspiration is his own creative vein. In the same way, his argument keeps faith with American sentiment about nature. To the metaphysical discourse of learned savants about the invisible world, he contrasts the ebullient energy of his character, Matthew Hobbs, one of those rural Jacks-of-all-trades who have given American science its dynamic individualism. The half-light of his workshop evokes the barns that Joseph Wright of Derby used to paint as well as Wright's own experiments in dynamics.

Judged by what is to come – a masterly series of works which unarguably illustrate Woody at his peak – the auteur in him has here found the inspirational cure he needed, turning a deaf ear to the annoying people who were giving him bad advice and following only his own clear, sound judgment.

*Midsummer Night's Sex Comedy*

The Expressionist power of these two women on the beach recalls Woody's own pictorial models.

Above: Emil Nolde: *Am Ufer* (*On the Bank*), water colour

*Interiors*

Group contrasts, profiles in silhouette: *Interiors* suggests, without imitating, the unsettling compositions of Eduard Münch.

**Above:** Eduard Münch: *The Room of the Dead*, lithograph, 1896.

In the elegiac *divertisse-ments* of summer, Woody's Impressionist vein evokes the picnics on the grass of Monet.

Above: Claude Monet: *Le déjeuner sur l'herbe*

*Midsummer Night's Sex Comedy.*

In this very Berg-
manesque setting, Tony
Roberts has the look of
Erland Josephson.

Rural escapade of a city dweller who can't stand the sun. *A Midsummer Night's Sex Comedy* is nonetheless a sequence of psychic vibrations and dazzling revelations, an ode to nature.

*Broadway Danny Rose*

# FROM WORDINESS

A protean figure, predisposed to continual metamorphoses: that's how Woody Allen has always been. Consider his film *Zelig* (1983). Although based on the idea of double camouflage (the butterfly camouflaged like a butterfly), it came along at just the right time to jog the memory of people who had been insisting for years that he repeat himself in one absolutely sure-fire box-office success after the other: 'Make a second *Annie Hall*!' This repeated demand must have had the same effect on him as that of the parakeet which used to say to André Breton: 'When are you going to write another *Manifeste* for us?'

Since the days when he wrote to order for other comics, through the times when he used to split himself roughly in two and fashion a movie myth (James Bond, Humphrey Bogart) as his alter ego, right up to the period that everyone scorned when he parodied the greatest film-makers, although only to reflect the torment that an auteur goes through, Woody has never stopped ringing the changes on appearance and language. He's progressed from the monologue and its shock-waves, from his beloved one-liners – which people continue to look for from him in his interviews (no doubt also the painful daily lot of Jules Renard and Oscar Wilde) – to the dazzling dialogue in which he often bequeaths to his co-star the first and last *bon mot*. He put words to the fore in his early films; next he turned the universe into a daily diary of events starring Brooklyn and Manhattan; finally he recorded his reluctance to deliver his seasonal 'fun film' by making – to the great distress of his own critics – his first film *without any gags*. Woody Allen has constantly asserted his autonomy, his right to remake or dismantle himself whenever he pleases.

With *Zelig*, he gave us a film without a label – one that resists classification. The first twenty-five minutes might make you think that it's simply going to be a series of static shots, photographed with little originality in black and white, based solely on narration derived from some rather vague case histories. In fact, what we have here is a super-production stuffed with trickshots which cost a fortune in research and archive material. We know now that the film represents three years' exhausting work; that it was shot while Allen was engaged on three of his other films, in experimental conditions that only a George Lucas could have afforded, surrounded by advanced technology and huge numbers of people. It's a strange film, the very opposite of his previous work, unique in its concept even if it seems to borrow from *Citizen Kane* the idea of the fake period documentary: instead of the *March of Time* Allen parodies certain kinds of television programmes like those of Kevin Brownlow on Hollywood, or the documentaries based on witnesses' testimony (of which *Reds* is an example).

A clinical and unemotional study of a curious case history – a totally fictitious one – based on the chameleon complex, the film recounts the imaginary life of an eccentric called Leonard Zelig who can transform himself on sight into virtually anyone: a black, an Asian, a Gentile, a psychiatrist, a fat man, a rabbi, in short everything that isn't Woody Allen but is what he might become in his unfilled moments, supposing he had any.

This experiment, performed on him with the help of hypnosis, is conducted by a specialist who has fallen in love with him, Dr Eudora Fletcher (Woody once had a headmistress of that name) played without noticeable glamour by Mia Farrow, this time exhibiting the unvarnished beauty of a Grant Wood. To the cure she brings the perseverance of an Alexander Graham Bell racking his brains to invent the telephone (here again one comes across Woody's fondness for the pioneer inventors). In order to succeed, Eudora Fletcher performs some bizarrely comic experiments and finishes up falling in love with Zelig and exposing his secret: 'It's safe to be like the others. I want to be liked.'

Little by little, the film assumes a structure, progressing from the display of trick effects to the story of a fictional analysis; at the same time the purely analytical, even condescending sort of documentary gives way to a serious, touching and revealing speech for the defence, which involves a kind of moral strip-tease and personal exorcism. Taking part in this pure piece of parody-collage are Woody's collaborators, themselves chameleons: Gordon Willis, the photographer, successfully reproducing the grainy effect of old newsreels; Dick Hyman, the composer, drawing inspiration from the kings of Tin Pan Alley; and 'witnesses' such as Susan Sontag, Saul Bellow and Bruno Bettelheim willingly sending themselves up as they come out with their theories about Zelig's obsessions. The whole effect shows the prismatic nature of celebrity and the fateful way in which renewal – that unalterable law of survival – can take place. For to become famous, one has to re-create oneself; yet renewal sometimes becomes the antithesis of celebrity, since the latter depends upon repetition. And *that* is the very theme of the film.

Notice that throughout all his transformations, unlike Alec Guinness, Woody stays stubbornly himself, while remaining like any one of us. *Zelig* is about the refusal to conform to the view of ourselves that other people claim to have or to the comic norms that they want to impose on us. Allen rejects that monstrous thing – conformity. He compares this mental passivity, this habit of knuckling under, to the most disreputable alibis for moral resignation. He physically attacks that submissiveness in the face of trendy fashions and theories; second-hand ideas which cause one to make intolerable allowances – even on behalf of Nazism. Woody trains his sights on intolerance from an unbelievably high rampart of scorn, in every way comparable to the way in which Chaplin, in *The Great Dictator* waged a world war against the archetypal tyrant. In his own fashion he attacks everyone who is a threat to his own existence – all the ayatollahs, the torturers, the purveyors of terrorism posing as holy war.

More modest than Welles (and as much of a genius) he has made a film that hides behind its own perfection. This superb jewel, labelled and displayed in the showcase, is the kind that dematerializes itself: it is both the diamond and the legendary drop of water, the grain of sand and the mirage-filled desert: it combines accomplished fact with a vanishing act.

Finally, like *Citizen Kane*, *Zelig* cannot be reduced to the documentary parody that begins the film and often dims it in

# TO WORDLESSNESS

the audience's memory. It is a cathartic achievement, an act of self-liberation which embodies, summarizes and concentrates the entire world of the film-maker. As with the human chameleon, Woody's versatility is his salvation. It is also his handicap as well as his refuge. Paradoxically, it supports his controversial status as a philosopher; it enables him to shift freely between entertainment and argument, to sidestep the occasional box-office failures and to turn a deaf ear to the demands of his critics. This immense achievement of Allen's renders him inviolate, snug at the heart of his own labyrinth. This prankish act of introspection, with its echo of 'I think, therefore I am', expresses the determination of a shy man, an alchemist who reduces an image to essentials, alters it and reconstitutes it before giving it wide currency and a hallmarked status. It's the only one of his films on which no illumination is shed by merely looking at the script: if one wants to assess the sub-text contained in it, like a watermark, one has to view it shot by shot.

The success of the film also springs from the way it avoids an excess of dialogue. Whatever the importance of the narration and even the sub-text of the narration (Woody the essayist is up to his cleverest tricks here) the sheer amount of imagery is staggering. For example, the scene with the multiple stethoscope, thanks to which a celebrated team of doctors examines a horizontal Zelig. Or the shot of Zelig, upright this time, but clambering up the walls and over the ceiling of the room like a crazy Babaouo.* These are gems of calculated looniness, latterday icons as 'true' in their way as certain photos by Robert Capa and Henri Cartier-Bresson.

Mad about magic, like Orson Welles, a fibber like Sacha Guitry in *Le Roman d'un tricheur*, and skilful at dissembling and creating illusions, Woody has invented the faked 'reality' which bestows a life of its own on what is counterfeit. It is with the Orson Welles of *Fake*, rather than with the creator of *Citizen Kane*, that he compares himself, even if it's from the latter film that he borrows the notion of the fake documentary at the start.

This time Woody seems to have perfected the blend of words and images. Each is continually counterpointing the other: the narration tells us what the image is hiding from us and the image entertainingly distracts us from the narration. At the same time, by making a film within a film – a sort of 'fiction squared' – in order to deny its truth or worth Allen suddenly seems to load his main story with a richness that leaves much still to be explored – a gold reserve whose source is some unknown factor of history or psychology.

Sometimes the narrator uses words to hint at events he prefers to leave undepicted: 'That day the doctors were experimenting with a midget and a chicken.' (One imagines some way-out monstrosity worthy of Tod Browning.) At other times he drops some totally irrelevant references into a very straightforward story. 'On his death bed, the only advice his father gives him is to save string.' He makes up Zelig-type jokes the way one used to tell shaggy dog stories; but at the same time, this is the first film in which Woody makes a determined attempt to dispense with dialogue. If *Annie Hall* and *Manhattan* represent the culmination of the monologue in the way he experiments with dialogue (those two forms that Woody has brought to perfection), *Zelig* decrees that dialogue shall be banished and includes a sub-text which illuminates

---

* Babaouo: the hero of a novel by Gaston Leroux which Salvador Dali wanted to adapt for the screen. Babaouo walked on the ceiling.

the story that the fake documentary throws into relief.

*Broadway Danny Rose* (1984), a return to straightforward story and pure comedy, also marks a return to verbal wit. It would seem to be a series of compromises. Indeed one can discern in it a deliberate retreat from autobiography. Danny Rose is no more an emanation of Woody Allen than Zelig is. From now on it will no longer be possible to see Woody as one used to be able to do – as a comic tired of making people laugh and oppressed by a world that's all too liable to dispirit him.

At the same time the film is the kind that tells a story. Woody even proposes what is, for him, a story of an original kind – a story told by someone else. After *Zelig*, which marked the abandonment of the first-person singular in favour of the third-person, and in which the hero 'broke into' the story, as it were, *Broadway Danny Rose* offers us yet another kind of narrative whose hero, presented as a third party and viewed with the unanimity of a Greek chorus, becomes part of everyone's collective memory.

In one of the story's very specific locations, the Carnegie Delicatessen (a sort of small European-style *charcuterie* monopolizing the meat-and-potatoes end of the market), we find an assembled *agora* of storytellers identified by their own names or ones they've assumed for the film. Entrusted to tell the story are such persons as Corbett Monica, Sandy Baron, Morty Gunty, Jackie Gayle and Howard Storm, Yiddish versions of a Manhattan Scheherazade, guaranteed to outdo each other in recounting events that improve as the story progresses according to the narrators' inventiveness. By such a device Woody relieves himself of responsibility: he no longer has to face the camera or find his way into the story.

All of them comics, these people evoke between them the legendary (and apocryphal) figure of the famous Danny Rose, a Broadway hero, the impresario of the has-beens, the stuck-in-the-ruts and the hopeless cases on the Avenue. Everyone has a story to tell about him. He is beyond price, inimitable, tireless, in such a way that before we see Woody appear in the part an 'entrance' has been prepared for him worthy of those which Sacha Guitry used to bring off in the days gone by. It bears repeating that this is no longer anything to do with Allan Stewart Konigsberg, the privileged resident of Central Park West, and a figure who symbolizes a smart and aware New York, but, rather, an artist's agent, admittedly a smart talker, who has a polished *spiel* and attempts to sell any act, especially those that are unsellable. Dressed sloppily and even in a rather period mode, he is an 'entertainer' of the kind John Osborne has described. Everything about him is hurried and brash, all clashing motifs, as if designed to make the eyes sore, thus eliminating the visual and accentuating the verbal, as one might paraphrase a famous song of the 1940s.

Danny represents dyspeptic crooners who sing of the pleasures of indigestion, one-legged tap-dancers, one-armed jugglers, blind xylophonists, nervous hypnotists who can't get their acquiescent victims to wake up, parrot trainers dressed up like Louis XV, skating penguins dressed like rabbis, adies who play tunes on crystal glasses . . .

The film shows Danny Rose threatened with murder, relying on his nimble tongue, surviving any and all tight spots (a kidnapping, a confrontation with the Mafia) by the dazzling ability to talk his way out – the power of words. Danny Rose is the perfect embodiment of Allen's sense of humour, a stammering sort of speech, enormously panic-ridden, coming from a man who has lived his life as if trapped on stage, between two shows, an endlessly interrupted monologue – in short, the nightmare of the stand-up comic at odds with the Borscht Belt.

Woody scatters Yiddish jokes, typical fare of the Catskill audiences, without finishing them, Jewish proverbs of didactic intent which are attributed to uncles invented on the spur of the moment ('My Uncle Menaghem . . . raised hamsters . . . My rabbi thinks we are all guilty in the eyes of God . . . My Aunt Rose . . . she used to say that you can't ride two horses with one behind', etc.). He makes use of marvellously meaningless phrases, deliberately wordy and turgid gobbledegook at odds with the situation: 'May I just interject one concept at this juncture? It's the classic pattern of a definitive situation. It's an entire mental syndrome,' and so on.

This remorseless flood of verbiage, whether coming from Danny (from whom Woody dissociates himself) or the storytellers at the Carnegie Deli, includes some oddities like the songs rendered by his partner Nick Apollo Forte: 'Agita', an ode to indigestion (as put into words by the stomach of a glutton) and 'My Bambina'. Note that the story is both characteristic of Woody, and yet not so. Danny Rose doesn't make his first appearance in the film in close-up as Alvy Singer and Ike Davis recently did, and is no longer given the last word. Danny remains the hero of a picaresque story told by first-class raconteurs – and the happenings leave them gasping and speechless. Woody leaves his gifted admirers bereft of words and prevents them composing an epilogue for him. It's unnecessary to add that *Broadway Danny Rose* is a tremendously funny film, with moments of pathos, which none the less contains visual delights, too.

These and many other successes led Woody to *The Purple Rose of Cairo* (1985), a film which impelled him to depart from his usual methods in a way that's surprising. Like an Escher engraving in which the rising curves blend with those descending, this film, stuffed with good things and the happy inventions of a highly active imagination, goes all out to challenge everything that's preceded it.

*The Purple Rose of Cairo* is the title of the film-within-the-film which is playing in a tiny, smalltown cinema in New Jersey right in the middle of the Depression. The players in the film are present at the (rowdy) screening of *The Purple Rose of Cairo* even though they are actors in it. Their existence is sanctioned by *The Purple Rose of Cairo* and will be transformed by it; players and audience participate in what happens in the film; and the film itself is influenced by the goings-on in the cinema. For the second time in his career, Woody doesn't appear once on the screen; yet it doesn't feel as if he is absent. His absence is a kind of tease: one thinks only of him, even though the film contains not a single self-centred auteur's gloss on his life or craft. Nevertheless, what it's about is illusion and reality. By forsaking an autobiographical approach, Woody takes a more considered look at the real influence he has over his work. Like Lewis Carroll's Cheshire Cat disappearing on the branch of a tree, Woody's smile hovers at the periphery of it. And his presiding authority is reinforced by the very disappearance of his usual method. In the absence of aphorisms and *bons mots*, the comedy is shaped by events, philosophy and poetry. Woody appearing by proxy, spoken for by others, as individuals or in the group, is nevertheless about as far as Woody can go in one of his major works.

The film's heroine, played by Mia Farrow, is a short-order waitress in the 1930s, crazy for the flea-pit cinemas, who escapes from her doleful milieu of New Jersey with its 1929

breadlines and her broken marriage by spending all her afternoons in a cinema, the Jewel, which is playing high-society comedies peopled with playboys in tuxedos doing the rounds of the night-clubs and speaking in the sort of sub-titles Anita Loos used to write. Her devotion pays off. One day the hero of that week's potboiler notices her from up there on the screen, speaks to her, climbs down, joins her in the auditorium and runs off with her, leaving the film in indescribable confusion. The consequences of this escape provide all the fun in a film based on the unpredictable, on the absurd, on the Piradellian nature of the situations. Woody at last advances beyond self-analysis and yields his place to the woman in love – and she, in her way, represents him completely. Cecilia, hopeless as a waitress, mixing up the orders, breaking plates and forever getting fired, daydreaming about life while waiting for the matinees at the Jewel, could, in other times, have been the soda-jerk Cecil, the weekly moviegoer, whom Woody himself played at the time of *Play It Again, Sam*. And indeed the film that she sees so often that she knows it by heart is to *Casablanca* what Cecilia is to Allan Felix, the hero of *Play It Again- Sam*. The players in *The Purple Rose of Cairo* put it explicitly when they say, 'We'll go to Casablanca, Tangier, Monaco or Egypt . . .' They really only walk through some very obvious studio sets; their journey matters less than the trip taken by Cecilia as she watches – liberated from the melodramas of the back kitchen and finding herself hobnobbing with countesses, explorers and men about town.

We very soon grasp the premises of this surreal film, a sort of nocturne. It carries us towards an unknown destination. (Whither are we bound? Which film will prevail over the other?) One feels one is at a lecture on 'The Transience of Reality', a magical trip into the cinematographic imagination and the cathartic effect it has on the real world. It's well known that the musicals of the New Deal era allowed the workless folk on 42nd Street to forget their helplessness: here the hapless waitress sees her Prince Charming coming out of a black-and-white film to inhabit a three-dimensional world. Like Alice, she will rejoin him on the other side of the mirror.

After fifteen years spent experimenting with language (images and dialogue inextricably linked by the priorities assigned to each in turn), Woody appears to have decided to advance beyond that point (beyond words) and to devote himself to simple narrative, spellbinding and riveting, which recalls the order given elsewhere by his producers – 'Give them a good story!' This modest squirrel who hoards his goodies like so many little nuts offers us, without vanity, boastfulness or the least hint of flamboyance, his own *Through the Looking Glass* – a real treasure among the timeless dreams that people weave.

This deliberate return to storytelling, forecast by *Zelig*, is achieved by a fable into which Woody has dissolved himself: the cinema's fiction has consumed his desire to appear in it. Such a fable about the illusory nature of reality had been attempted by no one before him, although Buster Keaton in *Sherlock Junior* had devoted one memorable sequence to illustrating the adventures of a flesh-and-blood person imprisoned inside the dynamic imperatives of a film. Woody does the opposite and depicts the surprises awaiting a film character who, emerging from his insubstantial universe, becomes aware of the most depressing reality of all, the Crash of 1929. Tom Baxter, the cliché explorer as he might be presented in a television series (in pith helmet and riding boots), thinks only in terms of clichés once he has descended from the screen, and is totally ignorant of life. Escorted by Cecilia, he wants to take 'a lesson in reality' and he discovers to his amazement that one may make love without having to resort to a 'fade-out'. The final pay-off doesn't leave Woody at a loss for invention: the film actor having been able to persuade his own image to reintegrate itself with the film, the people from Hollywood who had descended on the Jewel in a panic slink off back to their idiotic California (which Woody teases as much as ever) and leave Cecilia to the misery of her calamitous marriage – yet also in the stronghold of her dreams. The Jewel, where she very soon takes herself, is showing *Top Hat*. Astaire captivates the audience with his sublime sophistication and style. It is the Jazz Heaven out of *Stardust Memories* over again. And so one film begets another in the dual invasion of fiction by imagination, imagination by fiction. Woody, master of language and his world, fastens his seat belt and plots his latest flight-path.

Opposite and left: *The Purple Rose of Cairo*

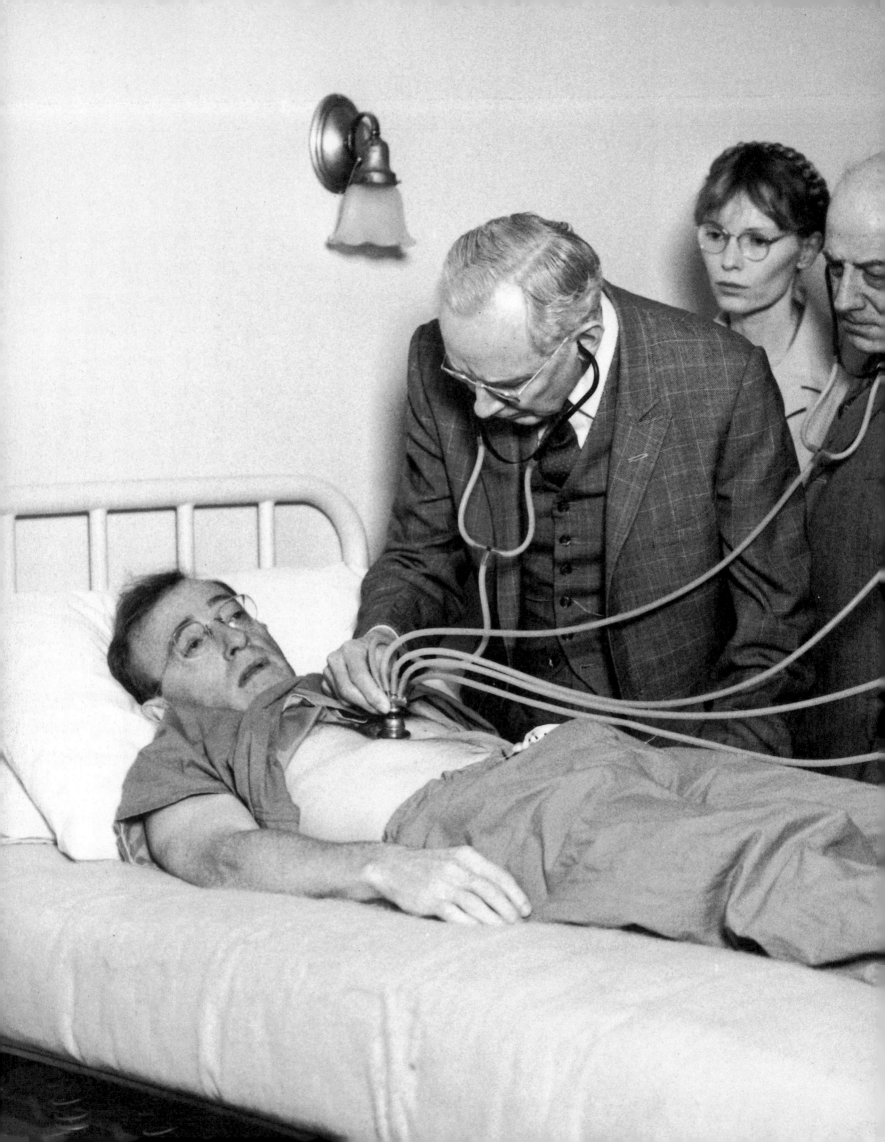

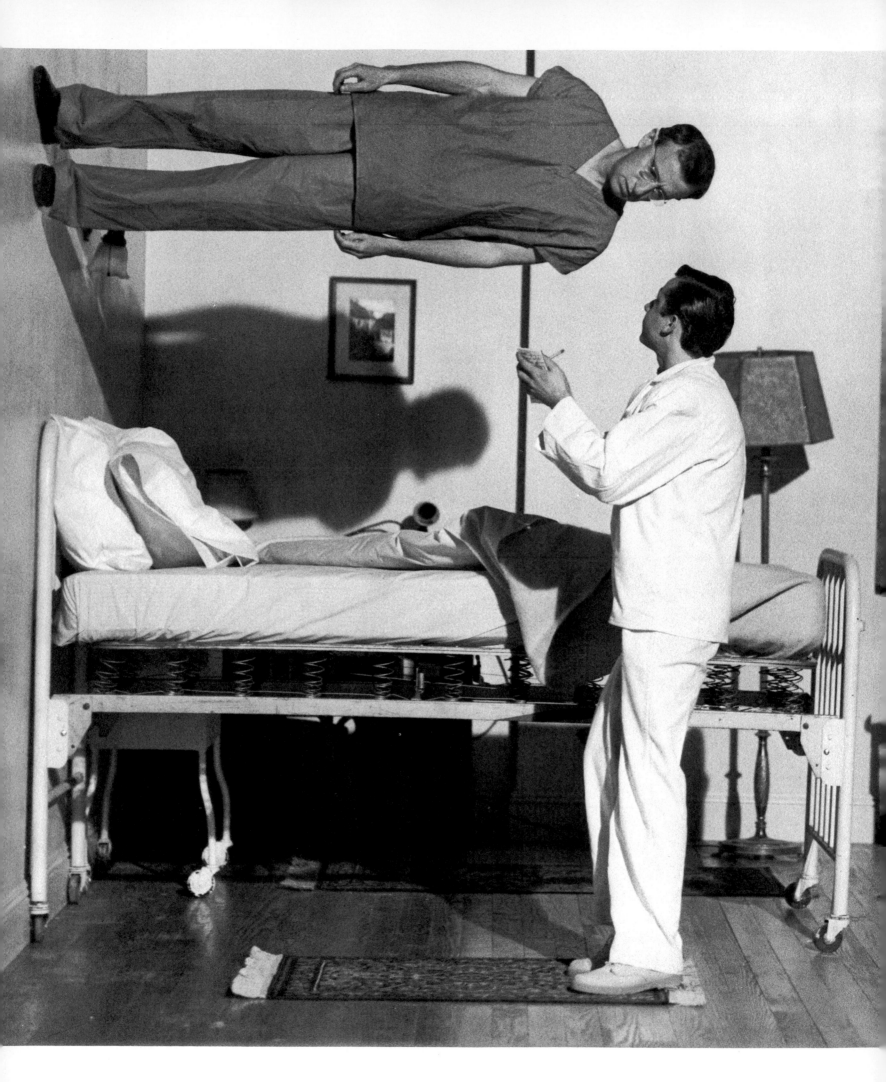

**Defiance as a theme in** *Zelig*: defiance of the body's integrity, defiance of gravity.

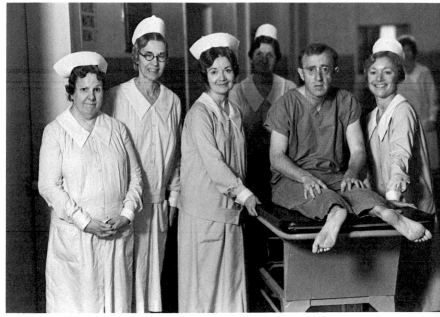

A forgery of genius (like Orson Welles in *Fake...* and in *Citizen Kane*). Woody creates the plausible in order to establish the unbelievable. *Zelig*, outwardly a documentary, establishes its fictional hero by surrounding him with famous people: Eugene O'Neill, Fitzgerald, Jack Dempsey, Calvin Coolidge, Herbert Hoover. *Zelig*

Tickertape welcome for
Leonard Zelig: the re-
incarnation fantasy of a
typical American hero,
Lindbergh. The com-
edian-hero of *The
Purple Rose of Cairo* will
realize his dream of
playing the role of
Lindbergh.

*Zelig*


Following page: stark-
ness of image and
meaning. An almost
Bressonian bareness of
image marks a high
point of expression in its
austerity.

*Zelig*

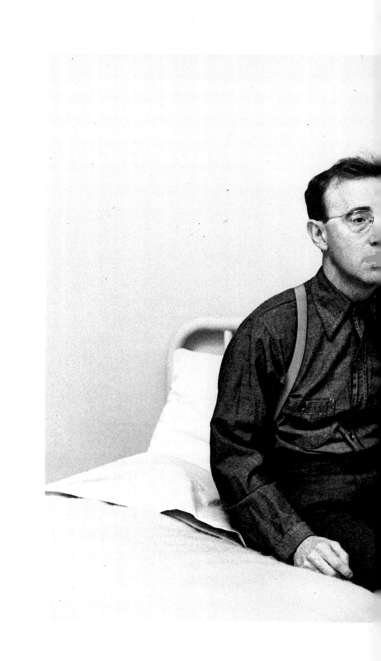

Deliberate *pointillisme*. Behind the glasses and the busy patterns of their apparel, Mia Farrow and Woody Allen resemble each other. Very shortly, she will be standing in for him.

*Broadway Danny Rose*

It's at the very time Woody takes leave of a style of film-making based on words that he inscribes on the cinema marquee five words of his film title. The metal letters loom above the heroine just as the fictional hero, up there on the screen, will descend on her.

Above: among the celluloid characters, there's one gatecrasher made of flesh and blood. Which one? Here, Woody mixes fact and fiction and, before long, sets them chasing each other all over the screen.

*The Purple Rose of Cairo*

Schnorrers
and Meshuggehs
**JEWISH**

'You don't have to be Jewish to be traumatized, but it helps'

**Woody Allen**

Woody Allen refuses to be pigeonholed in one rather constricted category, the American Jewish comedy. It is too racially based and characterized by the Borscht Belt routines with their jokes about mothers-in-law and rabbis.

He has created a comic universe which is both philosophical and autobiographical. He is the liberated Jew, free of complexes, quick-witted, detached from his basic image of frustrated *schlemiel*.

Yet his Jewishness remains an integral part of his comedy. He is neither Lester Townes (aka Bob) Hope nor James Bond, though he may have dreamed about the possibility.

He is unmistakably heir to an oral and literary tradition. He's the descendant of the Jews of Central Europe who fled the pogroms and the anti-semitic laws to emigrate to the USA. He illustrates the royal progress of the American comic who evolved out of the reception centres of Ellis Island and then scattered through the suburbs of Brooklyn and the 'Jewish Alps' (Catskills, Adirondacks). This was the birthplace of the *schtick* and the *tummlers* and the ethnic comic sketches which, from 1898 to the 1950s, enriched Broadway with dependable and well-lubricated routines which became more widespread and significant.

He succeeded, with his stammer and forgetfulness, in winning a place in that long line of entertainers stretching from Weber and Fields, Al Jolson, Harry Ritz and Eddie Cantor, Groucho Marx, Bert Lahr, Jack Benny, George Burns, Milton Berle, George Jessel, Danny Thomas, Sam Levenson and Phil Silvers through to Mort Sahl and Lenny Bruce.

The ethnic rebirth of American comedy couldn't have emerged from Hollywood, even though the latter was founded by Jewish magnates who built up the industry from the nickelodeons to the cinema circuits. Although the Jewish character had been depicted faithfully during the 1920s in many important films like *Humoresque, The Jazz Singer* and Capra's *The Younger Generation*, such was not the case at the start of the 1930s when the heads of the major studios, dissociating themselves completely from their ethnic background and origin, embarked on a systematic policy of social camouflage. Ben Hecht spelled it out in *A Child of the Century*, in 1954: 'Samuel Goldwyn, Louis B. Mayer, the Warner brothers, the Schenck brothers, Adolph Zukor, Harry Cohn, Irving Thalberg, Carl Laemmle, Jesse Lasky, and B.P. Schulberg wanted to bring about a camouflaged Jewish renaissance without rabbis or Talmud.' Indeed, apart from the series called *The Cohens and the Kellys*, which ended in 1933, the studios little by little threw a blanket of silence over the problems of the Jewish community. The subject was only broached in the form of drama, like *Crossfire* or *Gentleman's Agreement*. Hence the draining away of a kind of humour that went to enrich an entire series of productions, frequently 'underground' ones, like the Yiddish films of Edgar G. Ulmer, Joseph Seiden and others, which multiplied rapidly between 1932 and 1949.

If one were to try to trace the ancestry of Woody's comedy, one might distinguish three very clear branches: the English line, from Fred Karno (who gave Chaplin his start) to Stan Laurel and Andy Clyde, which came to a head in W.C. Fields, whose father was pure Cockney, and in Leslie Townes (Bob) Hope. The Irish line, from Mack Sennett to Buster Keaton, which resulted in Donald O'Connor and Red Skelton. Lastly, the Jewish line, astonishingly rich and widespread, takes in Chaplin, of English birth yet the incarnation, according to Hannah Arendt, of the Jewish outcast. After him, Larry Semon, Harry Ritz, Eddie Cantor, Groucho Marx, The Three Stooges, Danny Kaye, Jerry Lewis, Woody Allen, Mel Brooks, etc.

Allen was a thrifty boy, cosseted by his family, ensconced in the relative comfort ('intensely middle class', as he called it) of his surroundings. If one can credit it, he never suffered any bullying at school or got into any gang fights at street corners, which might have converted him, as it did Mel Brooks, into a pugnacious boy who could stand up for himself in violent abuse. Because he never had to suffer mistreatment or humiliation, Woody invented far-fetched and incongruous happenings in his early night-club routines: 'I was sent to an interracial camp for the vacation and introduced to smoking by kids of all denominations.'

In the Jewish world conceived by Woody there is something stimulating, warm and dramatic. In *Annie Hall*, Alvy's family dinner-table is quarrelsome, noisy and vulgar, yet packed with incident, a real eyeful: especially when compared (by means of the split screen) with the dinner of the Hall family, cold and correct, as if it had come out of a Norman Rockwell cover for the *Saturday Evening Post*. The Halls chew away silently at their meal, lips pursed, in glum, frozen postures, like a church meeting where every trace of humour has been suppressed. Humour for Woody often is a Jewish prerogative.

A highly literate man where the larger scheme of things is concerned, Woody feeds his mind by reading his friends: Singer, Bellow, Roth, Malamud, Heller and Salinger whose vivid language provides him with constant pleasure. In them he finds not only the echo of his own verbal zaniness, but also his neuroses and obsessions. (He offers his friends the latest Roth the way one proffers a box of cigars or chocolates.) And is he not the spiritual brother of their heroes, of Herzog, Gimpel, Portnoy, Fidelman and Yossarian?

# HUMOUR'S HIT-MAN

Top: in *Annie Hall*: Alvy the Orthodox Jew, as seen by Annie's grandmother. Above: contrast between the Jewish dinner-table and the Gentile meal at Annie's parents'.

In *Stardust Memories*, a rabinnical performance of *The Golem* anticipates the Hassidic troupe of Shakespearian players in *Zelig* (opposite).

**Spectacles as mask:** the unchanging accessory. For ten years, the same spectacles: face, features, hairstyle, clothes, everything changes except the spectacles. Even in a period film, they vouch for the contemporaneity of the character.

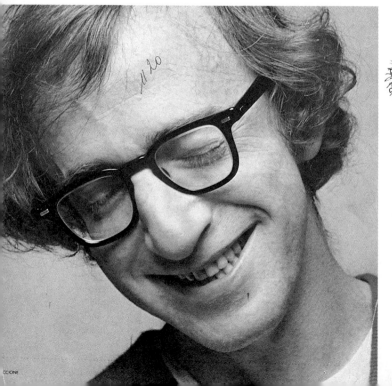

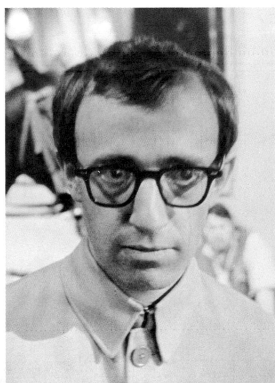

# A COMIC IN SEARCH

Not the least of Woody Allen's achievements is to stand the commonplaces of elegance and glamour on their heads: consider this unexpectedly photogenic safari outfit! He resists all stereotyping and expresses a unique image which defies every attempt to copy it.

There's Woody the awkward individual, a solitary chap, attached to the cosy little comforts of childhood (candies, comicbooks, Teddy bears, 'wax lips',* and boats in the bath): in short, Woody as he was at the start of his career. But beyond this deliberately unsophisticated appearance ('an untutored *nebbish*', Max Liebman remarked), there's an easygoing kind of guy who comes awake at nights and who, without following the fickle trendiness of fashionable New York, like the Andy Warhol crowd, for example, or the round of 'happenings', first nights on Broadway, private views at the Museum of Modern Art, has created a Manhattan for his own use, a movable environment whose private paths pass by Elaine's, Michael's Pub, the Russian Tea Room, John's Pizzeria on Bleeker Street and the poolrooms where he hides himself away during the previews that are to be avoided.

There exists another place of refuge for him – in a style and appearance that are typically Woody Allen and completely his own. It's a certain kind of sartorial 'go as I please', reflecting a taste for comfort: check shirts a bit on the big side, loose-fitting khakis and rumpled trousers, shoes that suit the rain, the recording studio or the running track: white buckskin with crepe soles, desert boots, slippers of the kind issued in hospitals and children's homes, footwear that's stout and built to last, without character but needing no care. One never sees him in patent-leather pumps, golf-shoes or any footwear with an Italian look. Nor is he to be seen in tennis shoes except when worn with a dinner jacket, as on the occasion of the celebrated Martha Graham gala. Though he's travelled in those European circles where co-productions flourish, he's never brought back home any tweeds, Fairisle sweaters or Yves St Laurent ties, but dresses himself like a hard-up kid on campus or some small-town professor.

Trenchcoats minus Bogey's bloodstains, rather shapeless out of choice, hats worn with brims turned down over thick-framed spectacles which give him a furtive appearance: the Greta Garbo look of the celebrity in perpetual flight. A fair exchange. From all this, he derives something of the individual flair with which he once endowed Annie Hall: he wears a hat a bit like the way she does and, like her, rejects the conventions of dress. In short, he's to be found under the 'circumflex accent' of his fedora – a profile in the true sense of the word, purveying his version of the distinguished personage on a medal.

And so one spies him: the quarry of show-business's dreaded *paparazzi*, in photos taken on the sly in among the restaurant tables (where, when the tribute can't be paid to him directly, they photograph his reflection in a mirror). Hand in front of his face or thrust out towards the lens (the ruses of a simple-minded fellow who throws himself into the water so as to avoid the rain and becomes a swimming champion), his face peeping

* Barley-sugar candy coloured red.

# OF HIS CAMOUFLAGE

Previous page: the Great Profile: Beady eye-glasses, a crocodile nose, a vaguely sinister felt hat – Woody manages to suggest a fashionable figure of dash and presence.

Hardly a rival to John Barrymore (one could call him The Great Little Profile), he projects an image both searching and serene.

In more than one respect, he brings to mind Snoopy in the *Peanuts* strip.

*Top:* Woody Allen at the O'Neill Theater, Waterford.
*Bottom: Stardust Memories*

out as if looking through a nervously opened door: Woody affects the appearance of a recluse only to discover he is a twentieth-century celebrity.

At home, despite his diffident disposition, he indulges a taste for boldly clashing materials: plaid shirts, Argyle socks on feet propped up on Persian or needlepoint cushions; and for trendy furnishings, a fourposter bed, table and commode in Early American style. If the public side of his life gives the strong impression of someone 'on the town', a metropolitan owl, his predilection for the transience of life is extremely sophisticated: the feeling of a captive air bubble has a priceless aura of permanence for him. At one time, Allan Felix of *Play It Again, Sam*, used to cry sardonically, 'I'm going to shower and douse my body with "Canoe"'! Nowadays, Woody invents a brand of perfume with a punning name: 'Proustian Rush'.* He has succeeded in doing inside a few years what poets like Francis Ponge or philosophers like Sartre or Lacan take a lifetime to do – reduce life to order and filter it to its essence.

Woody's preference for plain food over fancy cooking (he once spent a whole European vacation eating sole at every meal), his taste in simple and un-chic apparel, his scorn of the so-called essentials of urban living (he owns a Rolls-Royce but doesn't use it): all this adds up to his reputation with the campus crowd. In a cinema industry entirely aimed at prepubertal adolescents, his audience is, above all, that of educated but unpedantic youth, which mistrusts degrees and which, without actually identifying itself with him, hopes it will enter its forties so alert, so umblemished, so proof against compromise, so impervious to any intrusion into its private life.

This image has been created by Woody, whether intentionally or not, without publicist, agent, counsellors or lawyers even though he can, should he wish, consult any or all of them. He employs secretaries, but to do scarcely anything except help him avoid having to do anything not to his liking and keep nuisances away from him. Woody does everything, decides everything himself. Just the opposite of the comic whose celebrity has outrun him and who is powerless to catch up with life in the fast lane. His is a unique refuge in a show-business world where bodyguards, lawyers and fan clubs are the unbreakable rule.

To sum up, Woody represents all those freewheeling individuals who view the world afresh (not necessarily in their own image) like Edvard Munch, Stirner the nineteenth-century German philosopher, Gauguin, Mahler, Mark Twain, and Folon the poster designer. (Woody himself is like one of those 'living books' out of *Fahrenheit 451* who has his own responsibility to his art.) In short, he's like all those people who, by themselves, are progenitors of all the different parts of their universe, a world to which they give substance and of which they are the reflection.

In concluding this study, one has to view him as the offspring of his own *oeuvre*, a master of all disguises, a jealous protector of his own chosen solitude. Like the Chinese philosopher Wang Fu, he escapes into his own picture, fades from sight and vanishes. It's all in the picture: enquire within.

* Cf. *Stardust Memories.* DORRIE: That aftershave. It just made my whole childhood come back with a sudden Proustian rush. SANDY: Yeah? That's because I'm wearing 'Proustian Rush' by Chanel.

A rare and fantastic Woody making mock of a laid-back crooner, a Mafioso type in a black suit with boldly matching handkerchief and tie, the latter distinctly garish, as well as a cigarette held (rather wishfully) at a he-man's angle.

Dark glasses, nonchalant star: another picture of stylishness in *Stardust Memories*.

Snoopy (yet again!) versus the Red Baron or Formula One driver – the pilot's helmet signifying rash impulsiveness.

Left below: the beautiful people of *Annie Hall*: Annie and Alvy.
Right: Woody with Janet Margolin in *Take the Money and Run*.
Below right: Woody and Mia Farrow in New York City.

The wrinkled clothes designed by Ralph Lauren represent the exact opposite of the image Woody presented at first: everything that was once rumpled, outsize and ill fitting now assumes the glamorous trade-mark of the celebrity.

His turn to be the victim of the *paparazzi* (represented here by the leader of the pack, Ron Gallela). Woody turns into a furtive celebrity, protecting himself with his hat.

"I AM NOT THE DEBONAIR SEX BANDIT I MAY APPEAR TO BE.

**Woody as seen by the cartoonists.**

His major asset: a mobile face whose features are perpetually in search of an almost impossible inner peace. Drawings of him rarely focus on his body but, rather, on his features with special attention given to his glasses. Caricatures by David Levine (above) and Edward Forel (opposite, top)

...SO, YOU SEE, YOU ARE A UNIQUE INDIVIDUAL. NOW GO OUT AND BE YOURSELF.

FOR A WHILE THERE, I WAS ACTUALLY HAVING AN IDENTITY CRISIS...

# Three Conversations with Woody Allen

With its superb view over a chilly and denuded Central Park, this elegant Fifth Avenue penthouse resembles the movie-lover's cluttered pad in *Play It Again, Sam*, which is associated in our minds with Woody Allen's early style. Woody, pale and lunar, a courteous host, of impeccable manners, self-effacing to vanishing point, relaxes little by little amidst his comfortable furnishings and decor in which every object seems to have its specific place, set there with a sure and unostentatious good taste. On one big low table is an assortment of fruit, fresh and dried, raisins, cashew nuts, almonds, all placed on porcelain saucers and making an artistic picture of *nature morte*. During our conversation, this charming and diffident man punctuates his answers with little embarrassed laughs; he stammers; he utters *groans* of approval. Then as he gets into the interview, he becomes voluble, passionate, and finally expands in an unrestrained, even collusive way.

## On *Interiors*
9 December 1978
New York City

— **Ever since 1972, you have very often referred to the 'straight' movie you wanted to make — how you felt driven to do it and how it obsessed you. Did the form it finally assumed, set in a family during a severe crisis, owe anything to your admiration for O'Neill or Strindberg and their bleak kind of theatre?**

— Such ideas have been coming to me over the years. I personally knew a woman like Eve years ago and then, a little later, two sisters going through a difficult emotional crisis. It was at the back of my mind even while I was making several other films.

— **Does the need to make such a film spring from some of the criticism your comedies received, labelling them as too lightweight, close to making a statement, yet not doing so?**

—I've always felt that my first films were funny, but trivial; I found that my later films were also funny, but too derivative. One can say that about all my films. They are curtain raisers, entertainments and desserts: they lacked substance. I felt trapped in a dead end. Much as I enjoy a short of Chaplin's or Mack Sennett's, I made full-length comedies because I wanted to see if I could make people laugh for ninety minutes. Now I know I can do this.

— **Yet** *Love and Death* **didn't lack substance.**

— It's my favourite film. Even *Annie Hall*, which gave me real success, Oscars and everything, isn't as dear to me. But it's very hard to be as serious as you want to be within a comic film. People only see the laughter and don't remember the rest — they exit laughing and ignore the content. But if you do a completely serious film, you don't have to hide behind your laughs; it becomes a totally different experience.

— **The clowns in Shakespeare don't distract one from Hamlet; yet Hamlet wants to be a clown, and is not.**

— It's hard to do both things: one has to choose. Even Charlie Chaplin, who's the best comic of all, I think, would be very funny, but then he'd stop to be very serious. He could sometimes be both, but rarely. In all the many films he made, he did it only a couple of times, in *City Lights* or *The Gold Rush*.

— **Don't comics have a need for respect? Chaplin interrupted his films about the Little Fellow to do** *A Woman of Paris*. **Jerry Lewis stopped his career to do a film about concentration camps. After getting laughs, aren't comics anxious, at one time or another, to get admiration?**

— I think you get an enormous amount of respect out of doing funny films. But you want to do something different. It's like eating ice cream all the time; after a while, you need to take in something more solid. There are things that can be said only in a serious film. In *Interiors*, I felt freer than in my comedies. In comedies, people get most things at a superficial level. In O'Neill, in Chekhov, they receive things in depth.

— **I thought comedy was harder to construct than drama?**

— Actually, it is a little more difficult to do a funny film. People who deal with drama would like to do a funny film, but they simply don't know how. It takes a special kind of talent to make a comedy. When you see what great dramatic talents think is funny, well, it's not funny. But a comedian can sometimes do a serious film more easily. It's a strange talent to make people laugh. Of course you can work for a lifetime before you reach the level of a Bergman.

— **Some people say we already have a Bergman, but we've only got one Woody Allen. What do you think?**

There are so few comedians. On the other hand, I believe one's comedies will get better if one does a serious film now and then; and that's healthy. And I do enjoy serious films myself. When I grew up I had a preference for 'heavy' films, Antonioni, Resnais, Bunuel, especially Bergman.

— **I identify you more with the Scandinavians like Ibsen and Strindberg than with the Russians. Yet** *Love and Death* **is so Russian. Why do you and Mel Brooks love the Russian atmosphere so much?**

— It's a coincidence.

— **I understand the Russian streak in Mel. He was born Kaminsky and he loves Tolstoy, Lermontov, Gogol, and Dostoyevsky. But in you who were born Konigsberg I discern mostly the Northern streak, the metaphysical. Some scenes in** *Interiors* **look so much like a Munch painting, all those desolate beaches. You own a watercolour by Emil Nolde, a sketch by Kokoschka.**

— Yes, I love Sibelius, Wagner, Mahler and the German Romantics in literature. I'm true to my German origins. I am no sun lover. I am the opposite of Bernard Berenson who loved the Mediterranean culture. But I do appreciate the Russian milieu and when I shot *Love and Death* I found the Russians interesting because they were close to the subject I love. At the period in which the film was set, Russian intellectuals knew Romanticism and had an obsession with death, immortality, religion; they discussed Swedenborg the way Scandinavians do. To an American, they were an amusing ethnic and intellectual melange. Even today, Russians make me laugh, because they dress funny, because they are so square and, with their peasant faces, they're so intense, brooding, concerned with serious subjects, and humourless.

**— *Annie Hall* was your first movie in which you were completely grown up. Comedians like Stan Laurel, Chaplin, Langdon and Jerry Lewis had to play innocent, retarded, childish or neurotic people. You deliberately broke that mould by playing an adult with sexual hang-ups. Would it be possible, or even enjoyable, for you to come back to the old Woody Allen of *Bananas* or *Sleeper*?**

— No, the audience wouldn't believe in it any longer. In my new film, *Manhattan*, I also play a mere adult character.

**— Just as Chaplin once put 'a crease in his pants', so to speak, you left the clown behind and like Groucho Marx came to be what I call a joker in the style of the Renaissance jesters who were political and were used to plot and intrigue, but took definite stands.**

— Groucho was a master, a cynical, irreverent institution like American baseball. Trouble is, since the great wave of slapstick comedians, since Keaton and Chaplin and Langdon, the playing area has moved out of the realm of the physical to that of the psychological. All these artists came at the end of the industrial revolution and they expressed the physicality in everybody's life: we saw Keaton on his locomotive and Chaplin working on the assembly line. But now everything has become electronic and Freudian and the interest has shifted. The conflict is no longer about: Can I find work? Can I cope with nuts and bolts in a factory? It is: Can I stand the stress and pressure of working in an affluent society? The conflict is more subtle.

Ingmar Bergman has developed a new vocabulary on the screen to express the minds of people in a visual way: look at *Persona*, it is so visual. He makes the mind visual. It's very hard to express that in comedy. Even Chaplin today would have to do things more cerebrally, not just with his arms and legs. The screen comedian has to do funny things about emotional problems. You have to find new ways to do film comedy. I've been working on that ever since *Sleeper*. *Sleeper* was very physical, but it was not set *now*, in the present day. It took place in a more physical society. When I came to *Annie Hall*, however, I had to find ways to make the film express mental states visually and in a cinematic way. It's a non-physical film, but Diane Keaton, when she leaves her sentences uncompleted, does the opposite of what Chaplin would have done.

So I think we will have fewer clowns. Peter Sellers, for example, does marvellous things, but they don't ring a bell for adults. He's great when he does Inspector Clouseau, but you don't go home thinking whether it's important to your own life. Jerry Lewis is one of the great natural-born talents that I've ever seen; he's next to Charlie Chaplin for sheer natural gifts. His body, his voice, the way he moves, his level of craziness, what he does with language: he amazes me. Even today, if he comes on a talk show for five minutes as a mere guest and leads the band for one minute, he's absolutely great. His problem is he has not made good intellectual choices. If he did political satire, such as Chaplin did, even though he was accused of having intellectual pretensions, if he did social satire movies on the USA, he could be fabulous. Instead he aims lower than he should.

**By the way, you once said about the Marx Brothers that you first wanted your films to be slapdash and casual. Did you change your mind?**

— If you have to do that kind of energetic brash comedy, it has to be slapdash and unpretentious. But if you're trying to move, as I was in *Manhattan*, towards a sadder kind of comedy, where you have funny moments but a lot of sombreness too, you would have to use a deeper kind of direction. Slapdash melodrama would be pure melodrama, full of energy like *Mean Streets*, for instance, or *The French Connection*, two films I loved. But in the stylized drama you have to create a slower, more intimate feeling. Chaplin did it when he used all those close-ups, it was slower perhaps, but it was better comedy, more realistic, too. I like those scenes in foreign movies where nothing happens except someone is sitting there, eating, or walking. There is a wonderful scene in Bergman's *Cries and Whispers* where these people are eating, and it lasts for ever and is completely fascinating. In the USA you never see such things, there's always a demand for more action. This is indigenous to the USA where they want pace, fastness at all costs. As a result, we have melodramas, not dramas. We never get Ibsen or Chekhov; we get Lumet, Scorsese, Coppola, who are great but who usually do melodrama.

**You once said food was funny. Were you thinking in terms of giant carrots or lettuce, in terms of junk food?**

— No, food is funny in itself. It makes me laugh.

**— Incidentally, we are surrounded by food while we are talking.**

— I even thought of calling my Russian film *Love, Food and Death* or *Love, Death and Food*! I had a scene cut, which I shot in Paris, where Diane Keaton and I are on the way to assassinate Napoleon and stop at the home of a Jewish couple, at Yom Kippur, and eat a full dinner, only our plates have no food on them. It was very funny, but not usable.

**— You also had Napoleon being jealous of boeuf Wellington and wanting to have a dish named after him — eventually they gave him one, veal Marengo.**

— Here in the USA, we have a pastry called a Napoleon, which is really a *mille feuilles*!

**— In *Love and Death* all your supposed Russians are more likely Jewish intellectuals, eating blinis and behaving like American Jews. In *Interiors*, of all characters you seem to identify with Pearl, a nice person who laughs, is spontaneous and generous, the only character who seems to enjoy life. It isn't coincidental.**

— In *Interiors*, I identify with Pearl, Renata and Eve, and no religion is mentioned. In New York some people think that Eve, of all people, is the complete Jewish mother, that she has all the traits: compulsively clean, domineering, nagging, possessive with her children.

**— Do you believe in Jewish comedy, born from fear, aggressiveness, exaggeration, self-defence?**

— The truth is I grew up in a very Jewish neighbourhood, yet I never experienced in my life any kind of anti-semitism, I was never bullied at school because I was Jewish, I suffered no incidents, was never refused admittance, contrary to Groucho Marx in his well-known joining-a-club joke. I'm always surprised to meet someone who says I'm a

Jewish comedian. In over one hundred jokes I do, there may be one Jewish joke; it's like adding spice to a meal, but people will always say: you do so many Jewish jokes!

**– When you wrote gags for the radio, and you did fifty gags per day, how many were Jewish jokes?**

– In those days, you couldn't do them. I would put paper in my typewriter, write five jokes on each page then go home and there was nothing to it. In the 1950s jokes were about your wife, divorce, automobiles, but no Jewish jokes then.

It's true there is a certain aggressive wit in Jews. Chaplin is meaner, yet much funnier than Keaton. Keaton is a much greater film-maker, but not as funny. His films are great works of art, but when Chaplin just turns up at a street corner you laugh immediately. As for Groucho Marx he was simply the greatest comedian of his generation. And I relate to him as I would to a member of my family. Although W.C. Fields was a genius and decidedly gentile.

**– Is it true your mother looked like Groucho Marx, and is it why in** Take the Money and Run **you give the mother a Groucho Marx moustache?**

– It's absolutely true, and people always think I'm joking when I say this, but there is a family resemblance that I felt strongly. Especially when Groucho didn't wear his moustache, he looked like my mother's side of the family. As much as the Marxes themselves looked like each other. I met him at Lindy's Restaurant and it was exactly like meeting an uncle of mine, one of those uncles you meet at funerals or bar mitzvahs, and they shake hands with you, make a few nasty jokes, pinch your aunts or cousins, and nothing you do is right;

they're very sarcastic, but affectionate. Only I knew he couldn't have been my uncle. And my father looked like Fernandel! It was a very ethnic, lower-middle-class family, like a George Price cartoon, with clothes-pins and laundry hanging at the windows. Children were put out on the street at eight in the morning and played ball until eight at night.

**– Is it why you're so athletic? I'm told you could have made a career in sports?**

– I'm still very athletic today. At the minute we met I was back from playing tennis. That's all we did when we were young. We played in school yards, in ball fields, we played basketball, baseball, stickball, softball. I won track medals, could do all sports.

**– You acquired a real talent at sleight of hand.**

– I still do a few card tricks. When I was a boy I planned to become a professional gambler or make a career in crime! It seems all comedians can do a number of things like sleight of hand, photography, or play an instrument. Groucho played the guitar, Jack Benny played the violin like Chaplin, Sid Caesar the saxophone. I play the clarinet and soprano sax. There's a pattern it seems.

**– But you're a writer before everything. You had a gift for words even before you started to read books and acquire a culture.**

– It's true I like to write. I always had a real fascination for words. It's a gift you have from birth. I could always write easily; from the first grade I was the one who wrote things and read them aloud in class. I like it because it's quiet, you take your time and you do it alone. Making a movie is noisy, you have to work quick because you deal with fifty people. When you write something that you don't like you can throw it away. But a movie that you don't like you have to show, because people spent millions on it. When you write you don't have to meet the test of reality, while a film is never the ideal that you conceived. I write all the time. I give things to the *New Yorker* two or three times a year.

**– In fact you could have been part of the Algonquin Round Table. You relate to people like Perelman, Benchley or Ring Lardner – I'm thinking of his plays.**
– Benchley is hilarious. He had a way of making his best essays quite non-intellectual. I even love him as an actor. Things like *The Treasurer's Report* were never surpassed. And something like *The Sex Life of the Newt* could be right out of Dr Reuben.

**– Do you know the contemporary British 'absurdist' writers, people like N.F. Simpson or Spike Milligan?**
– I met Spike Milligan twelve years ago, and he still writes to me. He's quite crazy and I love him. When I was young on certain wave lengths I could get *The Goon Show*. Sellers and Milligan were terrific. Spike Milligan reminds me of our Jonathan Winters: complete craziness, uninhibited artistic madness, also the same level of mad despair.

— **How well do you remember the years when you wrote for Sid Caesar, with Carl Reiner, Mel Brooks and Neil Simon?**

— I mostly remember an infernal noise, everybody shouting like we were in a madhouse, fighting for our lines. Nobody had a lack of confidence. We worked like a kind of a steamroller. There were loud screams in the alley, then two of us would isolate in another room and write a page or two. Mel was the craziest of all, quite frantic. And yet the sweetest guy he still is to this very day. Mel is like Jerry Lewis, wrote for him. Both Jerry and Sid Caesar had the same hero. Once, I heard Sid mutter himself before group on stage: "Tonight I'm Harry Ritz!'" You know Mel Brooks he is much more popular than I am.

— **Do you still write plays?**

— They're putting on a board of directors to take over the Lincoln Center. I'm going to try and write plays for them. Lincoln Center will be another experience.* It's nothing like Broadway. I'll start with a comedy and if it works, I may get more adventurous.

*Sleeper*

**Magic**
The dream of sleight of hand, of levitation and of hypnotism.

*Stardust Memories*

* His first play at the Lincoln Center was *The Floating Lightbulb*, in 1981 (see Theatre section).

Care-worn and a little haggard behind his horn-rimmed glasses, rather palish and more strained than usual, Woody, wrenched from the relative peace and quiet of his New York terrace overlooking Central Park where the whole opening sequence of *Manhattan* was filmed, squares up to a fierce schedule of interviews and meetings in the salon of a grand hotel in Paris. He had thought while his latest film was opening in New York he would be able to give himself a week's vacation, *incognito*, in Paris – perhaps the first holiday in his career. For a long time he had wanted to take a stroll along the Left Bank and drop into a few cinemas. And then, suddenly! *Manhattan* was invited to Cannes and Woody

## On *Manhattan*

28 April 1979
Paris

**– You have stated that this film is about cultural junk food?**

– Yes, I think popular culture in America has become another kind of junk food; our television, our music, most of our films, our politicians, our architecture, most of it is very mediocre and junky. And it is too bad, because we have the money, the technical knowledge. We could have had the greatest culture, but people are drugged by television, by cocaine, by whatever.

**– Yet you yourself are a very cultured man, you have a great need for culture.**

– It's popular culture that really bothers me. What passes for 'good' and 'funny' and 'profound' on television and in the movies. I think *The Deer Hunter*, for example, is an unreal fake view of what happened in Vietnam. I don't think the war was about sadistic Vietnamese forcing poor Americans to play Russian roulette, but about American bombers dropping napalm on Vietnamese. If you care to do such films, fine – but when the Hollywood community honours it as the best film of the year, it is indicative of where American culture has gone to. Those American soldiers in that film could have as easily been trapped by a violent motor cycle gang — it said nothing about the war.

**– Haven't you become aware of all this because of the cultural experiences you yourself have absorbed? Now you've reached the point where you can't stand the superficiality of it all.**

– I am aware of the fact that at the close of the day there are no good movies to go to, you can't trust your politicians or walk down the street without seeing garbage. It is ridiculous to see America come to this; and it's not just New York, it's San Francisco, Detroit and all of the cities I know. In the film, Diane is an exponent of the fake intelligence: she plays a very neurotic intellectual indeed.

**– Which was what she played in** *Love and Death*.

– Except that there it was presented as a cartoon, so people went out laughing and didn't see anything more in it. This time I presented it as the real thing. She and her friend speak of an Academy of the Overrated, in which they put Proust and Mahler, and start out judging people who are real artists. They make their list, which is all right if it's a joke, but in the film they take it all seriously.

**– Is her list somehow like yours and, if not, whom would you put on your own list of the overrated?**

– Her list is quite different from mine, because in her

agreed to a couple of days of interviews of every kind with all the European press and television media. Spain, Holland, Germany, Britain, Switzerland, Denmark and Italy filed past him as, breaking with routine, he exposed himself to the curiosity of more critics than he had seen since his career began. He was politely explaining his film and the kind of role he played in it to people who hadn't seen it and wouldn't be able to see it before the Cannes Festival. He is wearing one of his favourite check shirts: he has had the same one, it appears, since his Broadway debut in *Play It Again, Sam* in 1969.

Academy there are many people I love; for instance, Norman Mailer, Scott Fitzgerald, Gustav Mahler. On my list I would put many venerated American film-makers that Europeans adore. I like many of our alleged great ones, but they're clearly overrated. They're nothing like Renoir or de Sica for example. They had great talent, did very entertaining films, but they are not thinkers.

**— Was the *Interiors* experience of 'going on a diet', so to speak, and doing a film without a gag profitable to you?**
– It was a wonderful experience. I was very glad of the way they received it internationally, because it's not a typical American movie – more psychological than active. Now I know what it's like to work one year on a very 'heavy' film. Like being in the army: it may be hard on you, but you learn from it.

**— Will you do this again? Another film without comedy?**
Yes.

**— You mean to maintain a balance between comedy and seriousness?**
– I tried to do it in *Manhattan*, which I believe to be a happy accident. I do my best to mix the two elements. But I don't think it came out as well as the critics said it did.

**— Can you time the need for**

**a joke to appear in a movie?**
– I can feel it in my body, and it feels good. For instance, there's the joke I did that Groucho Marx likes so much: 'I don't mind dying. I just don't want to be there when it happens.' My ambition is to do an entire film with nothing but jokes, like Bob Hope did.I tend to the classical, I like Greek classical art, simple and uncomplicated. When I see *Persona*, it seems perfect to me: two women, one speaks, the other doesn't; and yet, within this simplicity, it's a very intricate movie. I like that.

**— Is Manhattan still a dream city to you?**
– I get angry and frustrated when I think of it, but it's the same kind of frustration that you get when someone you love disappoints you. But in *Manhattan* I'm not critical of New York: I question the roots of it. It's not a movie that says 'Clean up Central Park'. It's a movie that says 'Clean up your emotional life, or you'll never be able to clean up Central Park'.

## On *Broadway Danny Rose*
24 January 1984
New York City

**– After shooting** *Broadway Danny Rose* **you're now doing** *The Purple Rose of Cairo:* **is there a connection between them?**
– None. It's just a coincidence.

**– Why this preoccupation with roses? Danny Rose in the film you've just shot sends a white rose daily to his beloved Tina Vitale (played by Mia Farrow). And you've had a very close collaborator, for a long time your best friend, who's called Mickey Rose.**
– Yes, Mickey Rose was my collaborator on *Bananas* and *Take the Money and Run*. We were students together and he moved to California. And I had white roses in *Interiors*, too.

**– In your next film, which is a fantasy, are you looking for something exotic from the past, perhaps what you once felt about the movie Casablanca?**
– There's nothing exotic in this film. It takes place during the Depression and deals with poor people who are out of work and, to kill time while waiting for something to turn up, keep going to the cinema to see a fictional movie called *The Purple Rose of Cairo*.

**–** *Zelig* **was a perfect balance between the visual and the verbal: isn't** *Broadway Danny Rose* **a return to the visual? Verbal comedy has always been a help and a hindrance to you. Is** *Broadway Danny Rose***, which you shot in a very free style, a way of levelling out both aspects?**
– Visual and physical are two different things. All my films are visual, including *Interiors*, which was drama. Whenever I don't use physical gags or slapstick, people cease to see visual structure in my films; but I have always been attentive to the visual side of them, even in my more talkative films.

**– Is** *Broadway Danny Rose* **(which, incidentally, is a very funny film) a way of giving in to all those objections of 'well-meaning' friends that you allude to in** *Stardust Memories* **who keep asking you to go back to 'those good old Woody Allen movies', those funny films they yearn for?**
– No!

**– By the way, the last one wasn't autobiographical. Obviously, you are not Danny Rose. He uses corny Jewish jokes and, if the people in the Carnegie Delicatessen admire him, it's because he belongs to the past.**
– It's true Broadway is very different from what it was when my father brought me there in 1941. That was before the honky-tonk people or the Mob took over. The people you met were more like Damon Runyon people. I used to go to the movies in 42nd Street, which is now a place left to hookers and pushers.

**– Ever since** *Stardust Memories* **you've taken an extraordinary interest in new faces, some deliberately grotesque. One sees quite a few of them in** *Broadway Danny Rose***. Is it true that you have what's been called a 'Woody Allen Task Force' and that you recruit or summon, the way Fellini does, people who have interesting faces? Or do you have staff who do that on your instructions and who know exactly what you want?**
– Yes, I have casting assistants from whom I request very precise types. They deploy themselves a bit everywhere, handing out 'open call' cards. My staff are used to my needs because they've been

working with me for years. I've had the same crew for something like ten years. On *The Purple Rose of Cairo*, too, except for Mel Bourne, who was hired for another film, but who gave me one of his collaborators because we have a lot of construction to do and I have a consistent idea about my sets from one film to the next.

— *Broadway Danny Rose* **was a fast, modest little film to shoot compared with** *Zelig*.
— *Zelig* was more expensive: it took three years to do, an arduous schedule with incessant technical experiment. Gordon Willis and I had to feel our way through some tough and complicated trick shots. *Danny Rose* is an improvised film, the way I like them. It was shot in the streets, on well-planned locations, and we wanted a rough-looking appearance which gave us lighting freedom – I didn't have to wait for the sun. Here I could shoot on the inspiration of the moment, call up my friends and shoot quickly in familiar locations. I've my little circle of favourite actors, or else I recruit others for the bit parts. In *Broadway Danny Rose*, I used Milton Berle. On *The Purple Rose of Cairo*, I almost used Diane Keaton, whom I would like to use along with Mia Farrow in a film. That would be very amusing, the two of them are so different. I've been able to bring together very different people like Van Johnson, Milo O'Shea, Jeff Daniels, and Dan Aiello who acted in my last play *The Floating Lightbulb*.

— **Your latest films have been made for Orion. Is it a happy collaboration?**
— The transfer of films from United Artists to Orion was effected for my own best interests. My next five films will be made for Orion. I lead exactly the same kind of life, I see the same friends, the same collaborators. I consider myself eminently privileged. I work as an independent, answerable to no one. If an idea strikes me as the seed of an interesting film, I start to work on it without provoking too much curiosity, and if I go wrong in a scene, I can do it over again without too much drama.

**1969**
**Take the Money and Run**
Technicolor, 85 mn.
*Directed by* Woody Allen; *screenplay:* Woody Allen, Mickey Rose; *produced by* Charles H. Joffe *for* Palomar Pictures; *executive producer:* Sidney Glazier; *associate producer:* Jack Grossberg; *director of photography:* Lester Schorr; *music:* Marvin Hamlisch; *artistic director:* Fred Harpman; *editing:* Paul Jordan, Ron Kalish; *set designer:* Marvin March; *costumes:* Erik M. Hjemvik; *special effects:* A. D. Flowers.
*Director of editing:* James T. Hecker; *musical director:* Felix Giglio.
*Cast:* Woody Allen (Virgil Starkwell), Janet Margolin (Louise), Marcel Hillaire (Fritz), Jaqueline Hyde (Miss Blair), Lonnie Chapman (Jake), Jan Merlin (Al), James Anderson (warden of penitentiary), Howard Storm (Red), Mark Gordon (Vince), Micil Murphy (Frank), Minnow Moskowitz (Joe Agneta), Nate Jacobson (the judge), Grace Bauer (the woman on farm), Ethel Sokolow (mother Starkwell), Henry Leff (father Starkwell), Don Frazier (the psychiatrist), Mike O'Dowd (Michael Sullivan), Jackson Beck (the narrator), Louise Lasser (Kay Lewis).
*Distributed by* XXth Century Fox.

**1971**
**Bananas**
De Luxe Color, 81 mn.
*Directed by* Woody Allen; *screenplay:* Woody Allen, Mickey Rose; *produced by* Jack Grossberg *for* Rollins and Joffe Productions; *associate producer:* Ralph Rosenblum; *executive producer:* Charles H. Joffe; *director of photography:* Andrew M. Costikyan; *music:* Marvin Hamlisch; *production designer:* Ed Wittstein; *editing:* Ron Kalish; *special effects:* Don B. Courtney; *sound:* Natan Boxer, James Sabat, Al Gramaglia; *musical director:* Felix Giglio.
*Cast:* Woody Allen (Fielding Mellish), Louise Lasser (Nancy), Carlos Montalban (General Vargas), Natividad Abascal (Yolanda), Jacobo Morales (Esposito), Mighel Suarez (Luis), David Ortiz (Sanchez), René Enriquez (Diaz), Jack Axelrod (Arroyo), Howard Cosell (himself), Roger Grimsby (himself), Don Dunphy (himself), Charlotte Rae (Mrs Mellish), Stanley Ackerman (Dr Mellish), Dan Frazer (priest), Martha Greenhouse (Dr Feigen), Axel

Anderson (tortured man), Tigre Perez (Perez), Baron de Beer (English Ambassador), Arthur Hughes (judge), John Braden (prosecutor), Ted Chapman (policeman), Dorthi Fox (Edgar Hoover), Dayne Crane (Sharon), Ed Barth (Paul), Nicholas Saunders (Douglas), Conrad Bain (Semple), Eulogio Peraza (interpreter), Norman Evans (senator), Robert O'Connell and Robert Dudley (FBI men), Allen Garfield (crucified man), Princess Fatosh (woman bitten by a snake), Dick Calliman (publicity man), Hy Anzel (patient).

*Distributed by* United Artists.

### 1972
### Everything You Always Wanted to Know About Sex but Were Afraid to Ask

De Luxe Color, 87 mn.

*Directed by* Woody Allen; *screenplay:* Woody Allen, *loosely inspired by the book of the same name by* Dr David Reuben.

*Produced by* Charles H. Joffe *for* Rollins Joffe and Brodsky-Gould Productions; *associate producer:* Jack Grossberg; *director of photography:* David M. Walsh; *sound:* John Strauss; *production designer:* Dale Henne Hennesy; *editing:* Eric Albertson; *director of editing:* James T. Heckert; *music:* Mundell Lowe.

*Cast:* Woody Allen (Victor, Fabrizio, the fool, the spermatozoon), John Carradine (Dr Bernardo), Lou Jacobi (Sam), Louise Lasser (Gina), Anthony Quayle (the king), Tony Randall (the operator), Lynn Redgrave (the queen), Burt Reynolds (the switchboard operator), Gene Wilder (Dr Ross), Jack Barry (himself), Erin Fleming (the girl), Elaine Giftos (Mrs Ross), Toni Holt (herself), Robert Q. Lewis (himself), Heather McRae (Helen), Sidney Miller (George), Pamela Mason (herself), Régis Phillips (himself), Titos Vandis (Milos), Stanley Adams (the stomach controller), Oscar Beregi (the brain controller), Alan Caillou (the fool's father), Dort Clark (the sheriff), Geoffrey Holder (the sorcerer), Jay Robinson (the priest), Ref Sanchez (Igor), Don Chuy and Tom Mack (football players), Baruch Lumet (Rabbi Baumel), Robert Walden (a spermatozoon), H. E. West (Bernard Jaffe).

*Distributed by* United Artists.

### 1973
### Sleeper

De Luxe Color, 88 mn.

*Directed by* Woody Allen; *screenplay:* Woody Allen, Marshall Brickman; *produced by* Jack Grossberg *for* Rollins and Joffe Productions; *associate producers:* Marshall Brickman, Ralph Rosenblum; *director of photography:* David

M Walsh; *editing:* O. Nichola Brown, Trudy Shipp; *artistic director:* Diane Wagner; *production designer:* Dale Hennesy; *special effects:* A. D. Flowers; *editing of special effects:* Ralph Rosenblum; *music:* Woody Allen, Preservation Hall Jazz Band and New Orleans Funeral and Ragtime Orchestra; *sound:* Jack Solomon, A. Gramaglia.

*Cast:* Woody Allen (Miles Monroe), Diane Keaton (Luna Schlosser), John Beck (Erno Windt), Mary Gregory (Dr Melik), Don Keefer (Dr Tryon), Don McLiam (Dr Agon), Bartlett Robinson (Dr Orva), Chris Forbes (Rainer Krebs), Maria Small (Dr Nero), Peter Hobbs (Dr Dean), Susan Miller (Ellen Pogrebin), Lou Picetti (the master of ceremonies), Brian Avery (Herald Cohen), Spencer Milligan (Jeb), Stanley Ross (Sears Swiggles), Jessica Rains (the woman in the mirror).

*Distributed by* United Artists.

### 1975
### Love and Death

De Luxe Color, 85 mn.

*Directed by* Woody Allen; *screenplay:* Woody Allen; *produced by* Charles H. Joffe *for* Rollins and Joffe Productions; *executive producer:* Martin Poll; *associate producer:* Fred T. Gallo; *director of photography:* Guislain Cloquet; *music by* Serge Prokofiev; *artistic director:* Willy Holt; *editing:* Ralph Rosenblum; *costumes:* Gladys de Seconzac; *special effects:* Kit West and Peter Dawson; *assistant directors:* Paul Feyder and Bernard Cohn; *musical director:* Felix Giglio; *sound:* Daniel Brisseau, Don Sable, A. Grimaglia.

*Cast:* Woody Allen (Boris Grushenko), Diane Keaton (Sonia Volonska), Georges Adel (old Nehamkin), Zvee Scooler (Boris's father), Despo Diamantidou (his mother), Olga Georges-Picot (countess Alexandrovna), Harold Gould (Anton Ledebkov), Jessica Harper (Natasha), James Tolkan (Napoleon), Howard Vernon (General Lévêque), Edmond Ardisson (the priest), Feodor Atkine (Mikhaïl), Henri Czarniak (Ivan), Yves Barsacq (Rimsky), Hélène Vallier (Madame Wolf), Lloyd Battista (Don Francisco), Harry Hankin (Uncle Sasha), Jack Lenoir (Kropotkin), Leib Lensky (Father André), Anne Lonnberg (Olga), Tony Jan (Vladimir Maximovich), Alfred Lutter III (the young Boris), Ed Marcus (Raskov), Denise Péron (the Spanish countess), Beth Porter (Anna), C. A. R. Smith (Father Nikolai), Shimen Ruskin (Borslov) Frank Adu (the recruiting sergeant), Tutte Lemkow (Pierre), Jack Berard (General Lecoq), Yves Branville (André), Eva Bertrand (woman in the lesson on venereal diseases), Brian

Coburn (Dmitri), Percival Russel (Berdikov), Jacob Witkin (Sushkin), Clément Thierry (Jacques), Chris Sandore (Joseph), Henri Coutet (Minskov), Alan Tilvern (the sergeant), Fred Smith, Glenn Williams (soldiers).
*Distributed by* United Artists.

## 1977
### Annie Hall
De Luxe Color, 93 mn.
*Directed by* Woody Allen; *screenplay:* Woody Allen, Marshall Brickman; *produced by* Charles H. Joffe *for* Rollins and Joffe Productions; *executive producer:* Robert Greenhut; *associate producer:* Fred T. Gallo; *director of photography:* Gordon Willis; *sound:* James Sabat, James Pilcher; *sound editing:* Dan Sable; *editing:* Ralph Rosenblum, Wendy Greene Brickmont; *production designer:* Mel Bourne; *animated sequences:* Chris Ishii; *costumes:* Ruth Morley; *production coordinator:* Lois Kramer; *production director:* Robert Greenhut; *songs:* « Seems like Old Times », by Carmen Lombardo and John Jacob Loeb, « It Had to be You », by Isham Jones and Gus Kahn, *performed by* Diane Keaton.
*Cast:* Woody Allen (Alvy Singer), Diane Keaton (Annie Hall), Tony Roberts (Rob), Carol Kane (Allison), Paul Simon (Tony Lacey), Janet Margolin (Robin), Shelley Duvall (Pam), Christopher Walken (Duane), Colleen Dewhurst (Annie's mother), Donald Symington (Annie's father), Helen Ludlam (Grandma Hall), Joan Newman (Alvy's mother), Mordecai Lawner (Alvy's father), Jonathan Munk (Alvy as a child), Ruth Volner (Alvy's aunt), Martin Rosenblatt (Alvy's uncle), Hy Ansel (Joey Nichols), Rashel Novikoff (Aunt Tessie), Russel Horton (man in cinema queue), Marshall McLuhan (himself), Dick Cavett (himself), Christine Jones (Dorrie), John Doumanian (drug addict), Bob Maroff, Rick Petrucelli (men in front of the cinema), Lee Callahan (cinema ticket seller), Chris Gampel (doctor), Mark Leonard (Marine officer), John Glover (actor friend of Annie), Ved Bandhu (Mahirishi), Dan Ruskin (comedian at rally), Johnny Haymer (comedian), Bernie Syles (comedian's manager), Lori Bird (Tony Lacy's girlfriend), Humphrey Davis (Alvy's psychiatrist), Véronique Radburn (Annie's psychiatrist), Robin Mary Paris (actress at the rehearsal), Jim McKrell, Jeff Goldblum, William Callaway, Roger Newman, Alan Landers, Jean Sarah Frost (Lacy's guests), David Wier, Keith Dentice, Susan Mellinger, Hamit Perezic, James Balter, Eric Gould, Amy Levitan (Alvy's classmates), Sigourney Weaver (Alvy's date at the

cinema), Walter Bernstein (Annie's date at the cinema).
*Distributed by* United Artists.

## 1979
### Manhattan
Black and white, 96 mn.
*Directed by* Woody Allen; *screenplay:* Woody Allen, Marshall Brickman; *produced by* Charles H. Joffe *for* Rollins-Joffe Productions; *executive producer:* Robert Greenhut; *production coordinator:* Jennifer Ogden; *production director:* Martin Danzig; *director of photography:* Gordon Willis; *sound:* James Sabat, Dan Sable; *editing:* Susan E. Morse; *chief set designer:* Mel Bourne; *costumes:* Albert Wolsky, Ralph Lauren; *music by* George Gershwin: « Rhapsody in Blue », « Love is Sweeping the Country», «Do-do-do», «S'wonderful», « Land of the Gay Caballero », '« Lady be Good », « Strike up the Band », « Embraceable You », *played by* New York Philharmonic *conducted by* Zubin Mehta.
*Cast:* Woody Allen (Ike Davis), Diane Keaton (Mary Wilke), Michael Murphy (Yale), Mariel Hemingway (Tracy), Meryl Streep (Jill), Anne Byrne (Emily), Karen Ludwig (Connie), Michael O'Donoghue (Dennis), Victor Truro, Tisa Farrow, Helen Hanft (guests at the party), Bella Abzug (guest of honour), Gary Weis, Kenny Vance (TV producers), Charles Levin, Karen Allen, David Rashe (TV actors), Damion Sheller (Willie), Wallace Shawn (Jeremiah), Mark Linn Baker, Frances Conroy (Shakespearean actors), Bill Anthony, John Doumanian (Porsche owners), and the dog Waffles.
*Distributed by* United Artists.

## 1980
### Stardust Memories
Black and white, 89 mn.
*Directed by* Woody Allen; *screenplay:* Woody Allen; *produced by* Robert Greenhut; *executive producers:* Jack Rollins and Charles H. Joffe; *director of photography:* Gordon Willis; *production designer:* Mel Bourne; *editing:* Susan E. Morse; *production director:* Michael Peyser; *artistic director:* Michael Molly; *sound:* James Sabat, Dan Sable; *costumes:* Santo Loquasto and Ralph Lauren; *make-up:* Fern Buchner; *songs and piano compositions, music adapted and performed by* Dick Hyman: « Hebrew School Rag », « Just One of Those Things », « Easy to Love »; « Tropical Mood Meringue », *written and performed by* Sidney Bechet; « I'll See You in My Dreams » *by* Isham and Gus Jones, *performed by* Django Reinhardt; « Body and Soul », *by* Edward Hyman, Robert Sour, John W. Green, *performed by* Lester Young *with* Count Basie and his orchestra;

« Three Little Words », by Bert Kalmar and Harry Ruby, *performed by the* Jazz Heaven Orchestra; « One O'Clock Jump » *by* Count Basie, *performed by the* Jazz Heaven Orchestra; « Brazil » *by* Ary Barroso and D. K. Russell, *performed by* Marie Lane; « Palesteena » *by* Russel Robinson and Con Conrad, *performed by the* Original Dixieland Jazz Band; « *A Night on the Bare Mountain* » *by* Moussorgsky, *performed by* the Vienna Opera Orchestra; « If Dreams Come True », *by* I. Mills, E. Simpson, B. Goodman, *performed by* Chick Webb; « Stardust », *by* Hoagy Carmichael and Mitchell Parrish, *performed by* Louis Armstrong.

*Cast:* Woody Allen (Sandy Bates), Charlotte Rampling (Dorrie), Jessica Harper (Daisy), Marie-Christine Barrault (Isobel), Tony Roberts (Tony), Daniel Stern (the actor), Amy Wright (Shelley), Helen Hanft (Vivian Orkin), John Rothman (Jack Abel), Anne De Salvo (Sandy's sister), Joan Neumann (Sandy's mother), Ken Chapin (Sandy's father), Leonardo Cimino (Sandy's psychiatrist), Eli Mintz (the old man), Bob Maroff (Jerry Abraham), Gabrielle Strasun (Charlotte Ames), David Lipman (George the driver), Robert Munk (Sandy as a child), Jaqui Safra (Sam), Sharon Stone (pretty girl on the train), Andy Albeck, Robert Friedman, Douglas Ireland and Jack Rollins (studio managers), Howard Kissel (Sandy's manager), Louise Lasser (Sandy's secretary), Sol Lomita (Sandy's accountant), Renée Lippin (Sandy's press assistant), Max Leavitt (Sandy's doctor), Irving Metzman (Sandy's lawyer), Dorothy Leon (Sandy's cook), Roy Brocksmith (Dock Lobel), Simon Newey (Mr Payson), Victoria Zussin (Mrs Payson), Frances Pole (Libby), Bill Anthony, Filomena Spagnolo, Ruth Rugoff and Martha Whitehead (fans at the hotel entrance), Judith Roberts and Barry Weiss (Sandy's partners in the « Three Little Words » sequence), Robin Ruinsky, Adrian Richards, Dominick Petrolino, Sharon Brous, Michael Zannella, Doris Dugan Slater (questioners at the screening), Stanley Ackerman (reporter at the screening), Noel Behn (Doug Orkin), Candy Loving (Tony's girlfriend), Denise Danon, Sally Demay, Tom Dennis, Edward Kotkin, Laura Delano, Lisa Friedman, Brent Spiner, Gardenia Cole, Maurice Shrog, Larry Robert Carr, Brian Zoldessy, Melissa Slade, Paula Raflo, Jordan Derwin, Tony Azito, Marc Murray, Helen Hale, Carl Don, Victoria Page, Bert Michaels, Deborah Johnson (fans in the foyer), Benjamin Rayson (Dr Paul Pearlstein), Mary Mims (Claire Shaeffer), Marie Lane (the cabaret singer), Gustave Tassel, Marina Schiano, Dimitri Vassilipoulos, Judith Crist, Carmin Mastrin (cabaret regulars), Sylvia Davis, Victor Truro, Joseph Summo, Irwin Keyes, Bonnie Hellmann, Patrick Daly, Joe Pagano, Wayne Maxwell, Ann Freeman and Bob Miranti (fans in front of the hotel), Cindy Gibb and Manuella Machdo (young girl fans), Judith Cohen, Madeline Moroff and Maurren P. Levins (friends of Sandy's sister), E. Brian Dean (policeman who arrests George), Marvin Peisner (Ed Rich), Robert Tennenhouse, Leslie Smith and Samuel Chodorov (autograph hunters), Philip Lenkovsky (the assassin autograph hunter), Vanina Holasek (Isobel's daughter), Michel Touchard (Isobel's son), Kenny Vance and Iryn Steinfink (the new studio managers), Frank Modell, Anne Korzen, Erik Van Falkenbourg, Susan Ginsburg, Ostaro Riggs, Wade Barnes, Gabriel Barre, Charles Riggs III, Geoffrey Friedman, James Otis, Judy Goldner, Rebecca Wright, Perry Gewertz, Larry Fishman, Liz Albrecht, Sloane Bosniak, James Harter, Henry House, Largo Woodruff, Jerry Tov Greenberg, Mahammid Nabi Kiani, Armin Shimmermann, Alice Spivak, Edith Grossman, Jacqueline French, John Doumanian, Jack Hollander.

*Distributed by* United Artists.

## 1982
### A Midsummer-Night's Sex Comedy
Technicolor Panavision, 87 mn.

*Written and directed by* Woody Allen; *produced by* Robert Greenhut *for* Rollins-Joffe Productions; *executive producer* Charles B. Joffe; *associate producer:* Michael Peyser; *director of photography:* Gordon Willis; *production designer:* Mel Bourne; *costumes:* Santo Loquasto; *editing:* Susan E. Morse; *sound:* James Sabat, Dan Sable; *casting:* Juliet Taylor; *production administrator:* Helen Robin; *artistic director:* Speed Hopkins; *animation effects:* Kurtz and Friends, Zander's Animation Parlour; *visual effects:* R. Greenberg's Associates; *credits and visual effects:* Computer Opticals Inc.; *set coordination:* Susan Kaufman, Toni Ross; *animals supplied by* Dawn Animals Agency Inc.; *production assistants:* Nicholas Bernstein, James Davis, James Greenhut, Nicole Holofcener, Joseph Pierson, Andrea Snyder; *make-up:* Fern Buchner.

*Music:* « Symphony no. 3 in A Minor » (« Ecossaise ») *by* Mendelssohn, *performed by* Léonard Bernstein and the New York Philharmonic, « Concerto for Violin in E Minor, Opus 64 » *by* Mendelssohn, *performed by* Vassili Stefanov and the TVR Symphony Orchestra, « Concerto Pour Piano no. 2 in D minor, Opus 40 » *by* Mendelssohn, *performed by* Eugene Ormandy and

the Philadelphia Orchestra, « Midsummer Night's Dream », *performed by* Eugene Ormandy and the Philadelphia Orchestra.

*Cast:* Woody Allen (Andrew), Mia Farrow (Ariel), José Ferrer (Leopold), Julie Hagerty (Dulcy), Tony Roberts (Maxwell), Mary Steenburgen (Adrian), with Adam Redfield, Moishe Rosenfeld and Timothy Jenkins (the students), Michael Higgins, Sol Frieder, Boris Zoubok, Thomas Barbour (the teachers) and Kate McGregor Stewart (Mrs Baker).

*Distributed by* Orion Pictures and Warner Bros.

## 1983
## Zelig

Black and white, 80 mn.

*Written and directed by* Woody Allen; *produced by* Robert Greenhut *for* Jack Rollins and Charles H. Joffe Productions; *executive producer:* Charles H. Joffe; *associate producer:* Michael Peyser; *director of photography:* Gordon Willis; *production designer:* Mel Bourne; *costumes:* Santo Loquasto; *editing:* Susan E. Morse; *sound:* James Sabat, Dan Sable; *casting:* Juliet Taylor; *artistic coordination:* Gail Sicilia; *production director:* Michael Peyser; *artistic director:* Speed Hopkins; *commentator:* Patrick Horgan; *choreographer:* Danny Daniels; *camera tricks:* Joel Hynick, Stuart Robinson, R. Greenberg Associates; *documentary research:* Mary Lance, Katie Meister, Dell Byrne, Jeff Goodman, Charlie Musser; *music and musical adaptation:* Dick Hyman; *photographic animation:* Steven Plastrill, Computer Opticals Inc; *photographs:* Kerry Hayes; *retouching:* Karen Dean, Judith Lamb; *make-up:* Fern Buchner, John Caglione; *original compositions by* Dick Hyman: « Leonard the Lizard », « Doin' the Chameleon », « You May be Six People », « But I Love You », « Chameleon Days », *performed by* Mae Questel, « Reptile Eyes », *performed by* Rosemary Jun; « The changing man concerts ». *Other songs:* « I've got a Feeling I'm Falling » *by* Harry Link, Billy Rose, Fats Waller, *performed by* Roz Harris; « I'm Sitting On Top of the World », *by* Ray Henderson, Samuel M. Lewis, Joe Young, *performed by* Norman Brooks; « Ain't We Got Fun », *by* Raymond B. Egan, Gus Kahn and Richard Whiting, « Sunny Side Up » *by* Lew Brown, B.G. De Sylva and Ray Henderson, « I'll Get By » *by* Fred Ahlert and Ray Turk, « I Love My Baby, My Baby Loves Me », « Runnin' Wild » *by* A. H. Gibbs, Joe Grey, Leo Wood, *all five performed by the* Charleston City All Stars; « A Surfboard in the Moonlight » *by* John Leob, Carmen Lombardo, *performed by the* Guy Lombardo Orchestra; « Charleston » *by* James P. Johnson and Cecil Mack; « Chicago, that Toddlin' Town » *by* Fred Fisher, « Five Foot Two, Eyes of Blue », *by* Ray Henderson, Samuel M. Lewis and Joe Young, « Anchors Aweigh » *by* George D. Lottman, Alfred H. Mile, Domenico Sanino and Charles A. Zimmerman, *all three performed by* Dick Hyman.

*Cast:* Woody Allen (Leonard Zelig), Mia Farrow (Dr Eudora Fletcher), John Buckwalter (Dr Sindell), Marvin Chatinover (endocrinologist), Paul Nevens (Dr Birsky), Stanley Sverdlow (dietician), Howard Erskine (doctor giving injection), George Hamlin (chemotherapist), Ralph Bell, Richard Whiting, Will Hussong (other doctors), Robert Iglesia (man at the barber's), Eli Resnick (man in the park), Edward McPhillips (Scotsman), Gale Hensen, Michael Jeeter (first year students), Sol Lomita (Martin Geist), Peter McRobbie (speaker at workers' meeting), Mary Louise Wilson (Ruth), Alice Beardsley (switchboard operator), Paula Trueman (woman on the telephone), Ed Lane (man on the telephone), Marianne Tatum, Charles Denney, Michael Kell, Garrett Brown (actors in *The Changing Man*), Sharon Ferrol (Miss Baker), Richard Litt (Charles Koslow), John Rothman (Paul Deghuee), Stephanie Farrow (Meryl), Dmitri Vassilopoulos (Martinez), Francis Beggins (speaker at town hall), Jean Trowbridge (Dr Fletcher's mother), Ken Chapin (interviewer), Gerald Klein, Vincent Jerosa (guests at Hearst's), Deborah Rush (Lita Fox), Stanley Simmonds (Lita's lawyer), Robert Berger (Zelig's lawyer), Jeanine Jackson (Helen Gray), Emma Campbell (Zelig's wife), Anton Marco, Louise Deitch, Bernice Dowis (plaintiffs), John Doumanian (Greek waiter), Will Holt (Adolf Hitler), Bernie Herold (Carter Dean); *with* Susan Sontag, Irving Howe, Saul Bellow, Bricktop, Dr Bruno Bettelheim, Prof. John Morton Blum (interviewed together), and Marshall Coles Sr (Calvin Turner), Ellen Garrison (Eudora Fletcher 80), Jack Cannon (Mike Geibell), Theodore R. Smits (Ted Bierbauer), Kuno Spunholz (Oswald Pohl), Sherman Loud (Paul Deghue 80), Elizabeth Rothschild (Meryl 80).

*Distributed by* Orion Pictures and Warner Bros.

## 1984
## Broadway Danny Rose

De Luxe black and white, 85 mn.

*Written and directed by* Woody Allen; *produced by* Robert Greenhut *for* Jack Rollins, Charles H. Joffe and Orion Pictures Productions; *executive producer:* Charles H. Joffe; *associate producer:* Michael Peyser; *production coordinator:* Helen

Robin; *production associate:* Gail Sicilia; *director of photography:* Gordon Willis; *production designer:* Mel Bourne; *costumes:* Jeffrey Kurkland; *editing:* Susan E. Morse; *sound:* James Sabat, Dan Sable; *casting:* Juliet Taylor; *music directed, arranged and scored by* Dick Hyman; *location coordinator:* Timothy Marshall Bourne; *make-up:* Fern Buchner; *visual effects:* Cinopticals. *Original music:* « Agita » and « My Bambina », *written and performed by* Nick Apollo Forte.
*Cast:* Woody Allen (Danny Rose), Mia Farrow (Tina Vitale), Nick Apollo Forte (Lou Canova), the comedians Sandy Baron, Corbett Monica, Jackie Gayle, Morty Gunty, Will Jordan, Howard Storm, Jack Rollins (in their own roles), Craig Vandenburgh (Ray Webb), Herb

Reynolds (Barney Dunn), Paul Greco (Vito Rispoli), Frank Renzulli (Joe Rispoli), Edwin Bordo (Johnny Rispoli), Gina Deangelis (Johnny's mother), Peter Castelloti (killer at the warehouse), Sandy Richman (Teresa), Gerald Schoenfeld (Sid Bacharach), Olga Barbato (Angelina), David Kissel (Phil Chomsky), Gloria Parker (virtuoso on glasses), Bob and Etta Rollins (ball act), Bob Weil (Herbie Jayson), David Kieserman (Ralph, owner of club), Mark Hardwick (blind xylophone-player), Alba Ballard (woman with the birds), Maurice Shrog (hypnotist), Belle Berger (hypnotised woman), Herschel Rosen (her husband), Joe Franklin (himself), Cecilia Amerling (fan in dressing room), Maggie Ranone (Lou's daughter).
*Distributed by* Orion Pictures.

## Acting, screenplay, additional direction

### 1966
### What's Up, Tiger Lily?
Eastmancolor-Scope, 79 mn.
*Screenplay and dialogue:* Woody Allen; *additional direction:* Woody Allen (*from the Japanese film* « Kizino Kizi » *by* Senkichi Taniguchi, *borrowed, copied, and with some original scenes*); *produced by* Reuben Bercovitch *for* Benedict Productions; *associate producer:* Woody Allen; *executive producer:* Henry G. Sapirstein; *production director:* Jerry Goldstein; *production designer:* Ben Shapiro; *stills:* Kazuo Yamada; *filming of additional uncredited sequences; editing:* Richard Krown; *credits:* Murakami-Wolf *for the* UPA; *songs:* « Pow » and « Pow Revisited » *by* John Sebastian, Joe

Butler, Steve Boone, Zalman Yanovsky and Skip Boone, *performed by* The Lovin' Spoonful, « Respoken », *written and performed by* John Sebastian, « Speakin' of spoken », *by* John Sebastian, *performed by* The Lovin' Spoonful; *traditional song:* « Fishin' Blues », *arranged and adapted by* John Sebastian, *performed by* The Lovin' Spoonful.
*Cast:* Tatsuta Mihashi (Phil Moskowitz), Miyi Hana (Terri Yaki), Eiko Wakabayashi (Suki Yaki), Eadao Nakamaru (Shepherd Wong), Susumu Karobe (Wing Fat), Woody Allen, The Lovin' Spoonful and China Lee (themselves).
*Distributed by* American International Pictures.

## Screenplay and direction

### 1978
### Interiors
Technicolor, 83 mn.
*Written and directed by* Woody Allen; *produced by* Charles H. Joffe and Jack Rollins *for* Rollins-Joffe/ Creative Management Productions; *executive producer:* Robert Greenhut; *production coordinator:* Barbara De Fina; *director of photography:* Gordon Willis; *production director:* John Nicolella; *editing:* Ralph Rosenblum; *chief set designer:* Mel Bourne; *costumes:* Joel Shumacher; *sound:* Nat Boxer, Bernie Hajdenberg, Jack Higgins; *make-up:* Fern Buchner; *music:* « Keeping out of Mischief Now » *by*

Thomas Fats Waller and Andy Razaf, *performed by* Tommy Dorsey; « Wolverine Blues » *by* John Spikes, Benjamin Spikes and Jelly Roll Morton, *performed by the* World's Greatest Jazz Band.
*Cast:* Kristin Griffith (Flyn), Mary Beth Hurt (Joey), Richard Jordan (Frederick), Diane Keaton (Renata), E. G. Marshall (Arthur), Geraldine Page (Eve), Maureen Stapleton (Pearl), Sam Waterston (Michael), Missy Hope (Joey as a child), Kerry Duffy (Renata as a child), Nancy Collins (Flyn as a child), Penny Gaston (the young Eve), Roger Morden (the young Arthur), Henderson Forsythe (Judge Bartel).
*Distributed by* United Artists

### 1985
### Hannah and Her Sisters
Eastmancolor, 107 mn.
*Written and directed by* Woody Allen; *produced by* Robert Greenhut; *executive producers:* Jack Rollins and Charles H. Joffe; *associate producer:* Gail Sicilia; *director of photography:* Carlo di Parma; *production designer:* Stuart Wurtzel; *costume designer:* Jeffrey Kurland; *editor:* Susan E. Morse; *casting:* Juliet Taylor; *production manager:* Ezra Swerdlow; *first assistant director:* Thomas Reilly; *second assistant director:* Ken Ornstein; *production co-ordinator:* Helen Robin; *script supervisor:* Kay Chapin; *assistant to Mr Allen:* Jane Read Martin; *production auditor:* Joseph Hartwick; *set decorator:* Carol Joffe; *set dresser:* Dave Weinman; *property master:* James Mazzola; *standby scenic artist:* James Sorice; *camera operator:* Dick Mingalone; *assistant cameraman:* Douglas C. Hart; *second assistant cameraman:* Bob Paone; *still photographer:* Brian Hamill; *additional photography:* Jamie Jacobsen; *production sound mixer:* Les Lazarowitz; *boom operator:* Linda Murphy; *sound recordist:* Tod Maitland; *re-recording mixer:* Lee Dichter, Sound One Corp; *make-up:* Fern Buchner; *hair design:* Romaine Greene; *men's wardrobe supervisor:* Mark Burchard; *women's wardrobe supervisor:* Patricia Eiben; *assistant to Mr Kurland:* Tom McKinley; *location manager:* Timothy Marshall Bourne.

*Cast:* Woody Allen (Mickey), Michael Caine (Elliot), Mia Farrow (Hannah), Carrie Fisher (April), Barbara Hershey (Lee), Lloyd Nolan (Hannah's father), Maureen O'Sullivan (Hannah's mother), Daniel Stern (Dusty), Max von Sydow (Frederick), Dianne Wiest (Holly), Lewis Black (Paul), Julia Louis-Dreyfus (Mary), Christian Clemenson (Larry), Julie Kavner (Gail), J. T. Walsh (Ed Smythe), John Turtarro (writer), Rusty Magee (Ron), Allen Decheser and Artie Decheser (Hannah's twins), Ira Wheeler (Dr Abel), Richard Jenkins (Dr Wilkes), Tracy Kennedy (Brunch guest), Fred Melamed (Dr Grey), Benno Schmidt (Dr Smith), Joanna Gleason (Carol), Maria Chiara (Manon Lescaut), Stephen Deflutter (Dr Brooks), The 39 Steps (Rock Band), Bobby Short (himself), Rob Scott (drummer), Beverly Peer (bass player), Daisy Previn and Moses Farrow (Hannah's children), Paul Bates (theatre manager), Carrotte and Mary Pappas (theatre executives), Bernie Leighton (audition pianist), Ken Kostigan (father Flynn), Helen Miller (Mickey's mother), Leo Postrel (Mickey's father), Susan Gordon-Clark (hostess), William Sturgis (Elliot's analyst), Daniel Haber (Krishna), Verna O. Hobson (Mavis), John Doumanian, Fletcher Previn, Irwin Tenenbaum, Amy Greenhill, Dickson Shaw, Marje Sheridan (Thanksgiving guests), Ivan Kronenfeld (Lee's husband).
*Distributed by* Orion Pictures

## 1985
## Purple Rose of Cairo

Technicolor, 81 mn.
*Written and directed by* Woody Allen; *produced by* Robert Greenhut *for* Jack Rollins and Charles H. Joffe Productions; *executive producer:* Charles H. Joffe; *associate producers:* Michael Peyser and Gail Sicilia; *production director:* Michael Peyser; *production coordinator:* Helen Robin; *director of photography:* Gordon Willis; *editing:* Susan E. Morse; *production designer:* Stuart Wurtzel; *costumes:* Jeffrey Kurkland. *sound:* James Sabat; *make-up:* Fern Buchner. *Original music:* Dick Hyman.

*Cast:* Mia Farrow (Cecilia), Jeff Daniels (Tom Baxter, Gil Shepherd), Danny Aiello (Monk), Irving Metzman (theatre director), Stephanie Farrow (Cecilia's sister), John Wood (Jason), Van Johnson (Larry), Deborah Rush (Rita), Zoé Caldwell (the Countess), Milo O'Shea (Father Donnelly), Dianne Wiest (Emma), Eugene Anthony (Arturo), Edward Berrmann (Henry), Karen Akers (Kitty Haynes), Annie Joe Edwards (Delilah), Camille Saviola (Olga), Peter McRobbie (the communist), Juliana Donald (the usherette), Ebb Miller (the conductor), David Kieserman (the owner of the cafeteria), Élaine Grollan (Victoria Zussin), Mark Hammond, Wade Barnes, Joseph G. Graham, Don Quigley, Maurice Brenner (the customers in the cafeteria), Paul Herman, Rick Petruchelli, Peter Castelloti (play promoters), Milton Seaman, Mimi Weddel (people buying tickets), Tom Degidon (ticket collector), Mary Hedall (popcorn seller), Margaret Thompson, George Hamlin, Helen Hanft, Leo Postrel, Helen Miller, George Martin, Crystal Field (filmgoers), Alexander H. Cohen (Raoul Hirsh), John Rothman (Mr Hirsh's lawyer), Raymond Serra (Hollywood patron), George J. Manos (the press agent), David Tice (the waiter), James Lynch (the head waiter), Sydney Blake (the reporter from *Variety*), Michael Tucker (Gil's agent), Peter Von Berg (the customer in the Drugstore), David Weber (photographic double), Glenne Headley, Willie Tjan, Lela Ivey, Drinda La Lumia (the prostitutes), Loretta Tupper (music hall owner).
*Distributed by* Orion Pictures and Warner Bros.

# Screenplay and acting

## 1965
## What's New, Pussycat?
Technicolor, 108 mn.
*Screenplay by* Woody Allen, *direction by* Clive Donner; *production:* Charles K. Feldman; *associate producer:* Richard Sylbert; *executive producer:* John C. Shepridge; *director of photography:* Jean Badal; *artistic director:* Jacques Saulnier; *credits:* Richard Williams; *music:* Burt Bacharach; *title song performed by* Tom Jones.
*Cast:* Peter Sellers, Peter O'Toole, Romy Schneider, Capucine, Paula Prentiss, Woody Allen (Victor Shakapopolis), Ursula Andress, Jess Hahn, Howard Vernon, Jean Parédès, Françoise Hardy, Douking, Daniel Emilfork, Annette Poivre, Louise Lasser, Richard Burton (not in credits).
*Distributed by* United Artists.

## 1967
## Casino Royale
Technicolor Panavision, 130 mn.
*Screenplay by* Wolf Mankowitz, John Law, Billy Wilder, Ben Hecht, John Huston, Val Guest, Joseph Heller, Terry Southern and Woody Allen; *inspired by the book of the same name by* Ian Fleming; *directed by* John Huston, Val Guest, Ken Hughes, Robert Parrish, Joe McGrath, *produced by* Charles K. Feldman and Jerry Bressler; *credits and editing of effects:* Richard Williams.
*Cast:* David Niven (Sir James Bond), Peter Sellers (Evelyn Tremble 007), Ursula Andress (Vesper Lynd 007), Orson Welles (The Number), Woody Allen (Jimmy Bond), William Holden, Joanna Pettet, Charles Boyer, John Huston (« M »), Barbara Bouchet, Jackie Bisset, Jean-Paul Belmondo, George Raft, Peter O'Toole, Stirling Moss, etc.
*Distributed by* Columbia.

## 1972
## Play It Again, Sam
Technicolor, 86 mn.
*Screenplay by* Woody Allen *after his play;* directed by Herbert Ross; *produced by* Arthur B. Jacobs *for* Apjac Productions; *executive producer:* Charles H. Joffe; *associate producer:* Frank Capra Jr; *production supervisor:* Roger M. Rothstein; *director of photography:* Owen Roizman; *sound:* Richard Pietschmann, David Dockendorf; *editing:* Marion Rothman; *music:* Billie Goldenberg; *additional music:* « Blues for Allan Felix », *written and*

produced by Oscar Peterson; « As Time Goes By », by Herman Hupfeld, song from the film « Casablanca », performed by Dooley Wilson.
Cast: Woody Allen (Allan Felix), Diane Keaton (Linda), Tony Roberts (Dick), Jerry Lacy (Bogart), Susan Anspach (Nancy Felix), Jennifer Salt (Sharon), Viva (Jennifer), Suzanne Zenor (girl at the discotheque), Diana Davila (girl at the museum), Marie Fletcher (Sharon in the dream), Michael Greene, Ted Markland.
Distributed by Paramount.

Almost his first complete film as auteur: only the direction wasn't his own. His whole universe is already present, including some privileged collaborators: Diane Keaton and Tony Roberts are on the starting line. His technical apprenticeship is beginning.

## Acting

### 1976
### The Front
Metrocolor, 95 mn.
Screenplay by Walter Bernstein; directed by Martin Ritt; produced by Martin Ritt for Jack Rollins and Charles H. Joffe Productions; executive producer: Charles H. Joffe; associate producer: Robert Greenhut; production coordinator: Lois Kramer; director of photography: Michael Chapman; sound: James Sabat, John B. Newman, Jim Stewart, Tom Beckert; editing: Sidney Levin; music: Dave Grusin; song: « Young at Heart », by Carolyn Leigh and Johnny Richards, performed by Frank Sinatra.
Cast: Woody Allen (Howard Prince), Zero Mostel (Hecky Brown), Herschel Bernardi (Phil Sussman), Michael Murphy (Alfred Miller), Andréa Marcovici (Florence Barrett), Remak Ramsay (Hennessey), Marvin Lichterman (Myer Prince), Lloyd Gough (Delaney), David Margulies (Phelps), Joshua Shelley (Sam), Norman Rose (Howard's lawyer), Charles Kimbrough (member of committee), M. Josef Sommer (president of committee), Danny Aiello (Danny La Gattuta), Georgann Johnson (T.V. interviewer), Scott Mckay (Hampton), David Clarke (Hubert Jackson), J. W. Klein (bank cashier), John Bentley (barman), Julie Garfield (Margo), Murray Moston (owner), McIntyre Dixon (Harry Stone), Rudolph Wilrich (private detective), Burg Britton (bookseller), Albert M. Ottenheimer (college principal), William Bogert (Parks), Joey Faye (waiter), Marilyn Sokol (Sandy), John J. Slater (T.V. producer), Renée Paris (girl in a hotel foyer), Joan Porter, Andrew and Jacob Bernstein, Matthew Tobin, Marilyn Persky, Sam McMurray, Joe Jamrog and Michael Miller, Lucy Lee Flippin, Jack Davidson, Donald Symington, Patrick McNamara.
Distributed by Warner-Columbia.

This is Woody Allen's sole appearance in a film of which he is not the auteur. Only the film's hard-hitting subject, an attack on McCarthyism, impelled him to accept what others had already set up (the film was co-produced by his agents), yet he found room in it for some of his own collaborators: James Sabat was to become one of his favourite technicians and Michael Murphy was to join Tony Roberts in playing 'best friend' roles.

### October 1969
Play It Again, Sam, produced by David Merrick; directed by Joe Hardy, with Woody Allen, Diane Keaton, Jerry Lacy, Tony Roberts. These four players were to repeat their roles in the film directed by Herbert Ross in 1972. Staged at New York's Broadhurst Theater, the play ran a year.

### 17 November 1969
Don't Drink the Water, produced by David Merrick with Jack Rollins and Charles H. Joffe at the Morosco Theater in New York; directed by Stanley Prager, designed by Joe Mielziner, costumes by Motley; with Lou Jacobi, Kay Medford, Anita Gillette, Tony Roberts, Dick Libertini, House Jameson, James Dukas, Curtis Wheeler, Gene Varrone, Olivier Clark, John Hallow, Sharon Talbot.
Adapted for the screen by Howard Morris in 1969, but with Jackie Gleason and Estelle Parsons in the leading roles.

These two plays occupy a vital place in Woody's career: Tony Roberts, who appeared in them, became his best friend and a privileged collaborator: the first play brought him the acquaintance of Diane Keaton, who became part of his life.

One-act plays, not staged: Death Knocks, Death, God, The Query.

### 21 April 1981.
The Floating Lightbulb, produced by Richard Crinkley at the Lincoln Center Theater, then at the Vivian Beaumont Theater, New York; directed by d'Ulu Grosbard, with Brian Backer, Eric Gurry, Beatrice Arthur, Danny Aiello, Ellen March, Jack Weston; design and costumes by Santo Loquasto.

# WOODY ALLEN AND MUSIC

A regular and inspired player of jazz (he puts in an appearance once a week at Michael's Pub, the New York City club where he plays the clarinet); a buff who is never stuck for an answer about the great moments in classical jazz; a constant admirer of the Big Bands of the interwar period (Tommy Dorsey, Glenn Miller, Harry James, Benny Goodman, Woody Herman, to whom, some say, he owes his adopted name) and whose music is often to be found on the sound tracks of his films: one can state that Woody Allen pays the same rigorous attention to popular music that Stanley Kubrick does to classical and experimental music.

His most personal films (*Manhattan*, *Stardust Memories*, *Zelig*) are imbued with pop tunes, jazz standards and hit-parade favorites, or else sultry orchestral arrangements from Armstrong ('Stardust'), Cole Porter ('Easy to Love') and George Gershwin to whom *Manhattan* seems dedicated.

Though he has recourse, for his classically funny films, to Prokofiev (*Love and Death*) or Mendelssohn (*A Midsummer Night's Sex Comedy*) and even to Moussorgski (for part of *Stardust Memories*), contemporary music and especially traditional jazz remains his chosen domain. His tastes in the matter of jazz range from the classical New Orleans of Louis Armstrong or Thomas Fats Waller and Sidney Bechet, the clarinettist on whose style he models his own, to Count Basie and Lester Young. In his very first film as an auteur, he had Oscar Peterson compose a blues number. He himself also composed the music for *Sleeper* and played it (astoundingly well) with the Preservation Hall Jazz Band and the New Orleans Funeral and Ragtime Orchestra. For him, music means something elegiac, nostalgic ('As Time Goes By') and votive. The scores to his films resemble concert programmes in their listings of titles, their references to innumerable complementary traditions and their fabric of nuances drawn from Dixieland, pop, Afro-Cuban, Harlem and 42nd Street.

## BIOGRAPHICAL DATA

Allan Stewart Konigsberg was born on 1 December 1935 at 142, 'K' Street in the Brooklyn suburb of Flatbush. Enroled at Midwood High School, around the spring of 1952 he began sending comic column-breaks to such columnists as Earl Wilson and Walter Winchell and got himself hired by David O. Alber Associates to write gags at $25 a week. At the same time he enroled at New York University, then at City College, from which he was suspended. Next, without taking a degree, he followed the communications media course of the Writers' Development Program funded by NBC TV. In 1953 he was earning $175 a week and, at the urging of the William Morris agency, writing comic sketches for Pat Boone, Buddy Hackett, Kaye Ballard, Peter Lindsay Hayes, Carol Channing and Stubby Kaye. He collaborated as a gag-writer on shows starring Ed Sullivan, Garry Moore, Sid Caesar and Art Carney. His two agents, Jack Rollins and Charles Joffe, then pushed him into performing on stage in his own routines: he made his first appearance at the Duplex, Greenwich Village, in 1961.

In 1965 he wrote the script for *What's New Pussycat?* and played his first screen role when the film was produced by Charles K. Feldman who re-engaged him as writer and performer for *Casino Royale* in 1967. In 1966 he 'recycled' a Japanese film, re-editing it and equipping it with brand new story and dialogue under the title *What's Up, Tiger Lily?* next he had his first plays staged on Broadway. *Don't Drink the Water* and *Play It Again, Sam*, opened on Broadway in 1969. He appeared in the film which Herbert Ross made of it in 1972. As they had forced him into cabaret, his two agents Rollins and Joffe made him turn his steps towards the cinema and in 1969 he directed the first film of which he was the auteur, or principal creator, *Take the Money and Run*. Rollins and Joffe, who have watched over his whole career, henceforth supervised the making of all his films as producers and collaborators and they have continued this relationship right up to the present.

From 1979 Woody Allen devoted himself completely to writing and directing his films, in which he nearly always took the leading role. He assembled a team of technicians (Gordon Willis, Mel Bourne, Susan Morse, James Sabat, etc.) and a 'family circle') of players (Diane Keaton, Tony Roberts etc.) on whom he could draw regularly for any of his films. This extremely fruitful period culminated in 1977 when *Annie Hall* won several Oscars; *Manhattan*, in 1979, affirmed his box-office appeal.

Woody Allen has appeared in numerous TV programmes, like *Hippodrome*, *Hot Dog* and *The Tonight Show* where he once replaced Johnny Carson. In 1971 he wrote and appeared in a show entitled *The Politics of Woody Allen: The Harvey Wallinger Story* for the PBS TV channel. This satire on Henry Kissinger was never broadcast. After that, Woody Allen turned his back on television and began contributing to numerous magazines such as *The New Yorker*, *New Republic*, *Playboy* and *Esquire*. The articles that appeared in their pages were later collected in book form (see Bibliography).

Woody Allen's ambitions as a filmmaker advanced with *Interiors* in 1978, in which he didn't appear and refused to make use of a single gag; then with *Stardust Memories*, in 1980, which he conceived as a declaration of independence. In it he reflected on the problems of creation common to some of the cinema's great artists (like Bergman or Fellini). Since *A Midsummer Night's Sex Comedy*, an 'entertainment' inspired by Shakespeare and others, he has formed a relationship with Mia Farrow, one of his 'stock company', and she has become his leading lady in subsequent films. He has brought her more and more to the fore and now seems satisfied to devote himself to direction. In *The Purple Rose of Cairo* he decided not to appear at all.

## BIBLIOGRAPHY

### Books about Woody Allen

Bill Adler and Jeffrey Feinman, *Woody Allen, Clown Prince of American Humor*, Pinnacle Books, New York, 1975.
Eric Lax, *On Being Funny: Woody Allen and his Comedy*, Hamish Hamilton, London, Elm Tree Books, 1976.
Giannalberto Bendazzi, *Woody Allen*, Castoro, Bologna, 1976.
Lee Guthrie, *Woody Allen, A Biography*, Drake, London and N. Y., 1978.
Michel Lebrun, *Woody Allen*, Pac, 1979.
Maurice Yacowar, *Loser Take All: The Comic Art of Woody Allen*, Ungar, New York, 1979.
Robert Benayoun, Vince Canby, Peter W. Jansen, Bert Koetter, Christa Maerker, Hans Gunther Pflaum, Hans Helmut Prinzler, *Woody Allen—Mel Brooks*, Reihe Film 21, Carl Hanser Verlag, Munich, 1980.
Miles Palmer, *Woody Allen, an illustrated biography*, Proteus, London and New York, Distr. Scribners, 1980.
Foster Hirsch, *Love, Death and the Meaning of Life*, McGraw-Hill, New York, 1981.
Gilles Cèbe, *Woody Allen*, Henri Veyrier, Paris, 1981.
Gérald McKnight, *Woody Allen: Joking Aside*, W. H. Allen, London 1982; Howard, & Wyndham, N.Y.

### Books by Woody Allen

*Getting Even*, Random House, New York, 1971:
Solar, Paris, 1973.
*Without Feathers*, Ballantine, New York: 1983
*Side Effects*, Random House, New York, 1980.

## DISCOGRAPHY

*Woody Allen*, volumes 1 and 2, Colpix CP 488, 1964–1965.
*The Third Woody Allen Album*, Capitol ST 2986.
*Woody Allen: The Nightclub Years, 1964–1968*, United Artists UA 9968, 1976.
*Woody Allen, Standup Comic, 1964–1968*, Casablanca, 1978–1979. A compilation disc which includes material from the earlier records.

## PHOTOGRAPHIC ACKNOWLEDGEMENTS

Some illustrations are from the author's personal collection.

AGIP, Robert Cohen
American Broadcasting Companies, Inc. © 1969
Apotheker
Camera Press, London: photo Alfred Gescheidt photo Fritz Schimke
Cavezzate
Christophe L
Cinemagence
Cinémathèque Française
Columbia: © 1965
Express: © 1975: photo Jean-Pierre Couderc
Forel, Edward: © 1976
Foto Parjetas, Madrid
Fotos International, Studio City, CA: © 1984
XXth Century Fox: © 1969:
Gallela, Ron: © 1978: © 1980, photo:
Gallela, Betty Burke: © 1983
Gamma, Warner Liaison
Giraudon, CFL
Gressard Gilles (Archives)
Hamill, Brian
Interpress
I.W.A. Enterprise, Inc.: © 1978
Lukovic, Jean-Pierre
Lambray, Maureen
Levine, David: © 1972
Magnum: photo Philippe Halsman: photo Ernst Haas Mark, Mary Ellen: Archive Pictures Inc. © 1979: Museum of Modern Art/Film Still Archive
National Film Archive, London
New York Times, photo John F. Urmiller
Newsweek
Orion Pictures Company: © 1978: © 1982: © 1983: ©: ©
Orkin, Ruth: © 1963
Oslo Kommunes Kunstsamlinger
Paramount: © 1972
Parimage
R.M.N., photo
Rollins & Joffe Productions
Stiftung Seebüll Ada und Emil Nolde
Team International
Transworld Feature Syndicate Inc.: photo Steve Shapiro
United Artists Corporation: © 1965: UA, © 1971 © 1972/: © 1973: © 1975: © 1977: © 1979 © 1980:
United Feature Syndicate
Warner Bros: © 1982 © 1983 © 1984 © 1985.